struggle to the summit

A true medical drama of providence and perseverance

Rivka Zucker
edited by Shaindy Perl

struggle
to the

ISRAEL BOOKSHOP
PUBLICATIONS

summit

A true medical drama of providence and perseverance

RIVKA ZUCKER
edited by SHAINDY PERL

Copyright © 2010 by Rivky Ludzker

ISBN 978-1-60091-119-4

All Rights Reserved

No part of this book may be reproduced in any form
without written permission from the copyright holder.
The Rights of the Copyright Holder Will Be Strictly Enforced

Book & Cover design by:

SRULY PERL • 845.694.7186

Distributed by:

501 Prospect Street, Lakewood, NJ 08701
Tel: (732) 901-3009
Fax: (732) 901-4012
www.israelbookshoppublications.com
info@israelbookshoppublications.com

Printed in the USA

Dedication

לזכר נשמת
הרב אברהם אליעזר
בן הרב **משה** ז"ל
ומרת **דבורה** בת **יעקב** ע"ה
ת. נ. צ. ב. ה.

*Dedicated in
loving memory by*
**Tuly and Tzippy Kaplan
and family**

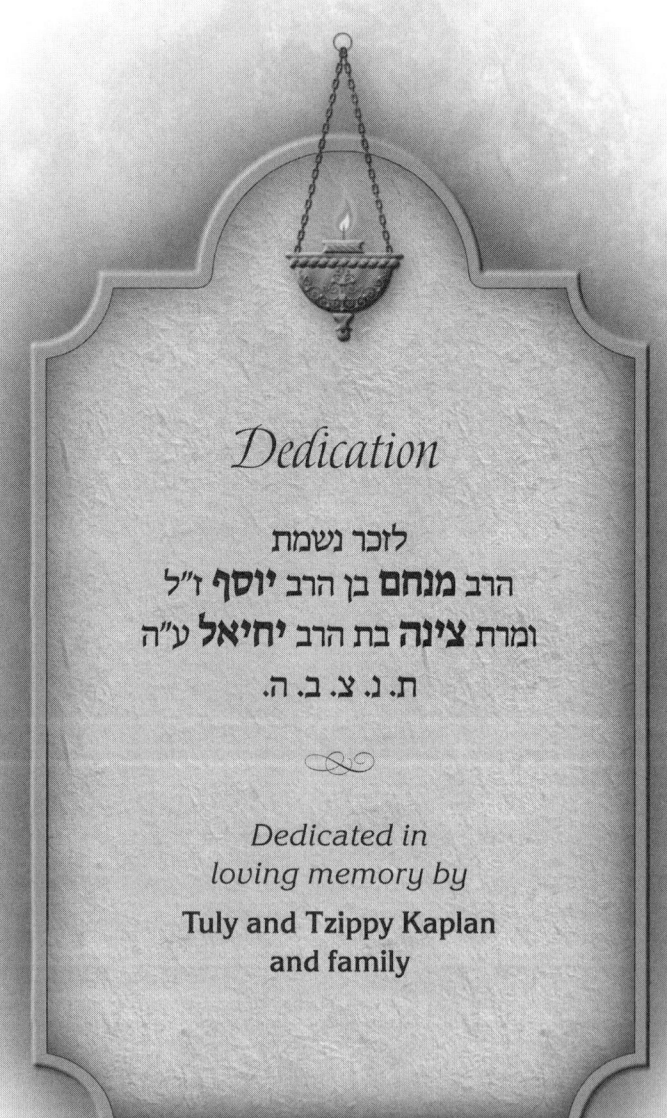

Dedication

לזכר נשמת
הרב **מנחם** בן הרב **יוסף** ז"ל
ומרת **צינה** בת הרב **יחיאל** ע"ה

ת. נ. צ. ב. ה.

*Dedicated in
loving memory by*
**Tuly and Tzippy Kaplan
and family**

Dedication

In loving memory
of our parents

ר׳ אפרים ב״ר שלמה ששון ז״ל

And our dear mother

מרת אסתר ב״ר יוסף ז״ל

Also our brothers and sister

ר׳ שלמה ב״ר אפרים ז״ל
ר׳ יוסף חי ב״ר אפרים ז״ל
מרת מזל טוב ב״ר אפרים ז״ל

Dedicated by the
Solomon family

Dedication

To the everlasting memory of

Solly and Lily Ludzker

עליהם השלום

who merited to see their offspring walking in the ways of the Torah.

Dedication

Dedicated in honor of
the esteemed doctors

Robert F. Spetzler, M.D.
and
Alexander Schick, M.D.

You were Hashem's special messengers whose medical expertise gave me a second chance for life. You both gave me hope and encouragement for a promising future.

With great appreciation,
Rivkah Zucker

ישיבה גדולה מאור יצחק
מאנסי נ.י.

אפרים שלמה וואקסמאן

I have been personally and closely acquainted with the Zucker family for many years. Their story is an inspiring tale of courage, *emunah*, and *bitochon*. They have faced daunting challenges with incredible fortitude and strength. The source of this strength has always been their deep connection to Hashem. This connection manifests itself not only in strength, but also in happiness, joy, and hope. Above all, Mrs. Zucker's fierce love and devotion to her family has sustained her and her family in a way that has moved and inspired all who have the privilege to know them. This story will remind us of what our true priorities in life are and it will teach us how to feel gratitude to Hashem for the gifts he bestows upon us.

Sincerely,

Table of Contents

Author's Note..15
Acknowledgements.......................................17
More Acknowledgements.............................21
Preface..23
1. Precarious Diagnosis...............................25
2. In Limbo..37
3. Arizona..43
4. Scenic View Rehab Center.......................53
5. Total Dysfunction...................................61
6. Life in 4A...75
7. Rehabilitation..95
8. Pesach Approaches...............................117
9. Sub-Acute Unit.....................................127
10. Home at Last......................................139
11. More Adjustments...............................157
12. Yomim Tovim.....................................171
13. Winter 2006-2007...............................185
14. One Year Post-Op...............................199
15. Spring 2007..219
16. Summer 2007.....................................233
17. Fall 2007..245
18. Winter 2007-2008...............................259
19. Two Years Post-Op..............................277
20. Independent at Last.............................291
    Epilogue..299
    Glossary..310

Author's Note

Dear Reader,

My objective in sharing my story is twofold. First, I want you to realize how lucky you are. Thank Hashem constantly when life seems ordinary or monotonous. Be thankful for normal inconveniences, such as staying up all night with a sick child or suffering from the common cold. Don't complain when your cleaning lady doesn't show up, you have a flat tire or your toilet clogs. Be thankful that you are able to stand and wash a sink full of dirty dishes, *schlep* the garbage outside, fold laundry, and bathe and dress your children. Though you may grumble as you perform these chores, for more than two years I yearned to do these ordinary tasks.

While I was going through my trying period, I was once speaking on the phone to a friend. She lived with her large brood of children in a small apartment on a *kollel* budget. Her life was challenging. Nonetheless, she told me that after discussing my situation with her husband, he told her, "Life just became easier."

That is my first message to you. Don't take your life for granted. Be grateful for the little things in life. Read my story, and life's challenges *should* become easier to manage.

My second goal in publicizing my story is to encourage those facing difficult circumstances. If you are also going through rehabilitation, for one reason or another, remember that it will take hard work to reach your goals. Be persistent until you triumph. Realize that it is *your* job to do your therapy; it is not up to the therapist to exercise for you. Trust me, I know it's difficult, but if you want to get to the top, it is up to you to climb the mountain. There may be guides and rails along the way, but there is no chairlift to carry you there.

I hope my story will give *chizuk* to those in a similar situation and will encourage anyone going through a difficult *nisayon*. Remember, Hashem does not give a person a *nisayon* he cannot handle. Use all the tools He has given you and persevere until the end. *Chazak V'ematz.*

Rivkah Zucker
August 2010

Acknowledgements

There are countless people to whom I am deeply grateful, for helping me in numerous ways throughout my recovery. I am extremely appreciative of all the wonderful women who visited me in the rehab center, keeping me company and helping me with my meals. I want to thank the Bikur Cholim volunteers, who brought me lunch every day and stayed to chat. In addition, I express appreciation to the women who came to play games with me and provided me with a social outlet while helping me improve my fine motor coordination.

I am especially grateful to a dear friend whom I have called Zehava Pearl in my story. She arranged my schedule of visitors while I was in the hospital and after I came home. She was always ready to assist with outstanding devotion.

I'm deeply grateful to the Ehrmann* family for extending themselves in support of my family during our ordeal. With neither set of parents living in town, the Ehrmanns adopted us as their own children. They hosted my children and allowed their daughters to act as mother's helpers on countless occasions. With incredible selflessness, they encouraged and aided us every step of the way.

I want to express my appreciation to my devoted friends Tzippi and Ruchala, who arranged suppers for my family and me. I must also thank my sister Hadassa, her

*Please note that the names of some medical institutions, doctors and other individuals have been changed.

friend Blimi, and my cousin Rivky, for keeping me sane by spending countless Shabbosos with me in the rehab center. Furthermore, I'm grateful to all the girls who spent Shabbos with my family, running my home when I was unable to do so.

Thank you to all those who provided assistance during my recovery and were inadvertently omitted. I am grateful for your kind support. I wish you *brochah*, and *hatzlochoh* in all that you do.

I must also acknowledge and honor Dr. Alexander Schick, a key player in my saga. Dr. Schick diagnosed my condition and, with total devotion, spent many sleepless nights researching a course of treatment for me. But he didn't stop there. After my operation, he phoned my husband on a daily basis for a whole month, to inquire how I was doing. Dr. Schick, I wish you many years of good health, success, happiness and *nachas*.

There are no words to convey how much I am indebted to the esteemed Dr. Spetzler of BNI at Saint Joseph's Hospital in Arizona. BNI is the most efficient and compassionate medical facility that I know. Dr. Spetzler is world-renowned for his expertise in the most delicate neurosurgery cases. If not for his willingness to risk his reputation and operate on a patient whom all other top neurosurgeons refused to accept, it's likely that I would not have survived. I owe him my life!

In addition, I want to show gratitude to Dr. Robbie Ofir who worked with me and taught me for over two years. Robbie imparted his vast wealth of knowledge to me as an instructor of the Feldenkrais method.

Acknowledgements

Most of all, I am eternally grateful to my wonderful husband, Yisroel, who stood by me throughout my ordeal. He spent countless hours researching my options, and he ultimately made all the decisions regarding my medical care. He lovingly pushed and guided me in the right direction throughout my rehabilitation. If not for his encouragement and support, I never would have accomplished as much as I did, during my recovery.

Finally, I would like to convey my deepest gratitude, and praise to *Hakadosh Boruch Hu* for holding my hand as I confronted my life's greatest challenge. He guided me and sent many *sh'luchim* to aid me, as I made an almost impossible trek up an exceedingly steep mountain. I thank You for sustaining me and bringing me to where I am today. I pray that I will merit to raise my children in health and happiness and to *shep nachas* from them together with my husband, *ad meah v'esrim shana*.

More Acknowledgements

On another front, I want to thank those who worked with me and helped bring my dream of publishing my story to fruition.

First and foremost, I give my editor, Shaindy Perl, the biggest *yaasher koach* for taking my manuscript and formatting it into a book. Shaindy, you are an incredibly talented and gifted writer. You are a master at writing others' perspectives through interviews. I am very impressed with how dependable you are. I truly enjoyed working with you.

To my dear sister Leeba: I cannot even begin to express my gratitude for the countless hours you spent on my book. Leeba, I can see you as a professional editor in the future.

I want to thank Liron Delmar of Israel Bookshop who pointed me in the right direction from the start, providing me with constructive criticism and helpful tips and ultimately getting me in touch with Shaindy Perl.

I must acknowledge Mrs. Shami Reinman, who taught me in high school. She gave me lots of encouragement and pointers on getting my book published. May Hashem grant her many years of good health and allow her to keep giving to others.

I would like to express my appreciation to my mother, Mrs. K., and Mrs. Eva Gruenebaum for tediously reading through my manuscript and correcting errors.

I am also grateful to all those who read through my writing over the last few years and gave me their valuable input and opinions.

I want to thank my generous sponsors, who helped me cover the expense of publishing my story. They get part of the *zechus* in helping me give *chizuk* to others.

Finally, I wish to thank the *Ribono shel Olam* - the healer of all flesh, for bringing me to where I am today and for giving me this opportunity to share my story of *chizuk*.

Preface

I wrote the following poem, in December 2006, when I was in complete physical dysfunction and in a desperate state. It appeared in Binah Magazine on March 5, 2007.

Dear Hashem,
I have a yearning and longing,
And aching within;
To recover and be
All that I've once been.
To be able to walk,
Use both hands with ease,
To take care of my children;
I beg of you please!
I want to change diapers,
Do laundry and dishes,
Be wife to my husband,
Fulfill all his wishes.
Clean chickens, scrub toilets,
Peel potatoes, mop floors,
Take out the garbage,
And organize drawers.
Give my kids baths,
And then brush their hair.
Tuck them in bed,
And do all their care.
It's hard to sit by,
To observe and to see,
Others doing my job,
When it should really be me.
Hashem please help,
Make my progress move fast,
Restore me my health,
And make this all past.
And when I am better,
And able again.
I hope to do more,
Than I ever did then.
I plan to keep busy,
With many good deeds.
For the past ten months,
I've planted the seeds.
I pondered and thought,
Turned ideas in my mind.
I just want to go,
And leave this behind.

STRUGGLE TO THE SUMMIT

To be whole and complete,
Is to what I aspire,
But Your help, Hashem,
Is what I require.
I'm doing all I can,
To get to my goal.
I ask and I beg,
Please make me whole.
No therapist or doctor,
Can promise a cure,
But You can, Hashem,
And of that I am sure.

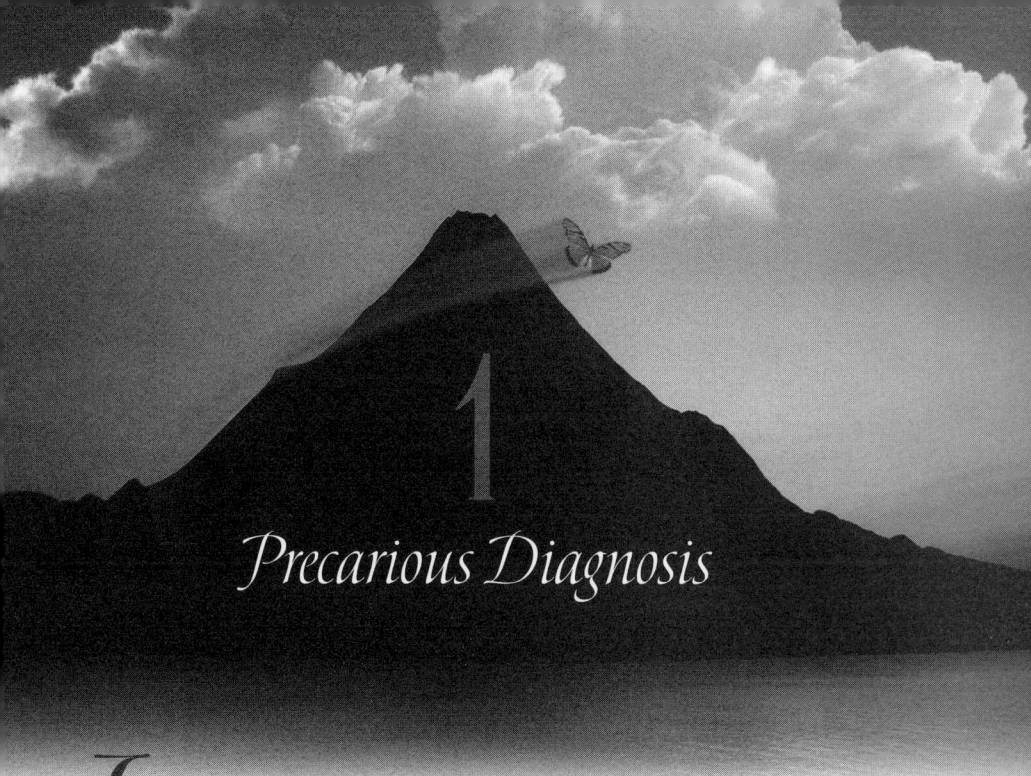

1
Precarious Diagnosis

In the middle of December 2005, around a year before writing the "Dear Hashem" poem, I was thirty years old and leading an active, fulfilling life. Everything seemed picture perfect. I was happily married to a wonderful husband and, I was a stay-at-home mother to two beautiful young children: nineteen-month-old Libby, and six-month-old Shloimy.

My family had recently moved into our own home in Monsey, New York, and purchased a pre-owned minivan for me to drive. Chanukah had just passed, and I had organized a family get-together in our house. Life was good and I was content.

At the time, I had been experiencing something bizarre for quite a while, but I was so busy, that I paid little attention to it. It actually started four years earlier, when I had taken a trip overseas. While putting on lip liner, I had noticed that the left side of my lip felt funny and tingly. I didn't realize that it indicated anything serious.

Though I had planned to see my doctor once I returned home, the funny sensation went away. I figured I had probably pinched a nerve while sleeping in an awkward position on the plane, so I didn't think a visit to the doctor was necessary.

I didn't have any odd sensations again until a couple of years later, during my second pregnancy. The tingling came back and lasted for about three weeks. Worried, I went to the doctor, and he performed various blood tests to rule out conditions such as Lyme Disease and Epstein-Barr Virus. The tests came back negative, and the funny sensation went away, so the doctor told me not to worry about it. (I later learned that he suspected I might have Multiple Sclerosis, but he did not want to distress me during my pregnancy, especially, since there was nothing I could do about it then.)

In October 2005, when Shloimy was three months old, the strange sensation returned and lasted for about three months. This time the tingling developed into numbness and spread around my mouth and half of my tongue. This worried me, but since I had a dentist appointment scheduled after Chanukah, I decided to discuss it with the dentist during my appointment.

During my visit, the dentist could not tell me the cause of the problem, but he informed me that I was feeling symptoms from two separate facial nerves. This caused me to be more concerned, since it meant that it wasn't merely a problem with one isolated nerve. I realized that I was dealing with a much larger issue, and knew I should see a doctor immediately.

About a week after the dentist visit, on a Shabbos afternoon in January, I was relaxing with my husband while the children napped. We were chatting together, when I suddenly let out a deep, long sigh. "What's gonna be?" I asked.

I am an optimistic person by nature, so my husband was quite surprised at this uncharacteristic question. What was giving me that feeling of dread? I couldn't explain the sudden sensation that gripped me, but I just knew something was going to happen.

The next day, Sunday, I planned to join a local Jewish library. The library was located in the basement of a *shul,* and I knew I wouldn't manage alone with both children. I left my toddler, Libby, at the home of a close family friend, Zehava Pearl, and drove with the baby to the library. When I arrived, I had a difficult time maneuvering the new minivan into a parking spot. "I guess I am not used to the dimensions of the vehicle yet," I thought.

After I finally parked, I opened the back hatch with the automatic button and removed the Snap N' Go base for Shloimy's car seat. I fumbled as I awkwardly tried to unfold it. When it was finally open, I took Shloimy with his car seat out of the car and placed it into the base. Once again, I struggled to snap it into place.

At last, I walked into the *shul,* and headed towards the long flight of carpeted steps leading to the library downstairs.

As I bumped the stroller down each step, I felt as though I was about to fall. I kept grabbing the handrail for support.

When I finally reached the bottom, I faced a large room that was crowded with people and surrounded by bookcases. Suddenly, I felt disoriented and couldn't see straight. I was gripped by a strange sensation, and I felt compelled to leave immediately. Though I had wanted to become a member for some time now, I made an abrupt about-face.

Going up the stairs was more challenging than coming down; I had to walk up backwards and pull the stroller in front of me. I wished someone would offer to help me, but I looked like I was in the best of health. No one could see how I was actually feeling. I couldn't even put my finger on what was wrong. I just didn't feel right.

"What is happening to me?" I thought in panic. "Something is dreadfully wrong. I think there's a problem in my brain. Maybe I have MS!"

I drove back to Zehava to pick Libby up. Every time I turned a corner, my car went a little too far, forcing me to make a wide turn to get into the street. I assumed that something was wrong with the steering wheel of our new minivan.

When I reached Zehava's house, she was surprised to see me at the door. "That was quick," she said. "I wasn't expecting you back so soon."

"Something is wrong," I told her. "I don't feel right, so I turned back immediately. I think something is wrong with my brain."

Precarious Diagnosis

A look of concern crossed her face. "What do you mean? What do you think is wrong?" she asked.

"Something bad," I said. "I'm afraid to say."

I packed up the kids and drove home. The rest of the day I continued to feel strange. I was clumsy and disoriented, and my speech was stilted as well.

When my husband came home that evening, I told him what I was experiencing, and he called his doctor, Dr. Cohen. My husband had been using Dr. Cohen for years, and he trusted his opinion. After he explained my symptoms, Dr. Cohen responded that they were signs that could indicate a stroke. "Take her straight to the emergency room," he ordered.

I thought that my husband had exaggerated my symptoms, so I took the phone and explained how I truly felt. "Come right over," Dr. Cohen said, "and I'll examine you."

Dr. Cohen's office is located on the same street as his house, so even though it was Sunday evening, he was able to meet me there right away. Since I felt too unsteady to drive myself, my husband drove me. Dr. Cohen led me into the examination room and performed a full neurological and coordination exam.

"You are not having a stroke," he informed me when he was done, "but you must see a neurologist and have an MRI of your head as soon as possible."

"Will I live through the night?" I asked. I wanted to gauge the seriousness of the situation by watching his reaction.

"Yes," he replied. "With Hashem's help, you'll be fine."

Dr. Cohen advised me to see a neurologist named Dr. Schick, who worked in Beth Israel Hospital in Manhattan. I scheduled an appointment for the following Monday, when my husband would be able to take off from work. I did not realize the urgency of seeing the neurologist that same week.

Since Dr. Cohen was not my primary care physician through my insurance, I still had to visit my primary doctor for a referral. My husband could not take off from work, and I had to manage the appointment on my own. I couldn't possibly go with two babies, so I left Libby with Zehava and brought Shloimy to the doctor with me. Once again, driving was awkward, and I struggled with Shloimy's car seat in and out of the car.

After my doctor examined me and discussed my symptoms, she prescribed an MRI for me and gave me a referral to Dr. Schick, the neurologist Dr. Cohen had recommended.

Over the course of the week, I became increasingly uncoordinated. I had a hard time walking straight, and I bumped Shloimy into the wall a few times as I carried him. I also couldn't pour a drink without spilling some of it. Moreover, I felt drained and awfully fatigued. I did manage to take care of some minimal grocery shopping, cooking and childcare, but it was clear that something just wasn't right. I spent most of the day sitting in the rocking chair with Shloimy on my lap, as I watched Libby playing on the floor.

When I awoke on Friday morning, my entire left arm felt tingly, as though I had slept on it. The sensation lasted throughout the day. This additional symptom worried me, so

Precarious Diagnosis

I called my husband. He contacted Dr. Cohen, who instructed him to take me directly to the emergency room, preferably at Beth Israel Hospital in Manhattan. "Make sure they take an MRI of your wife's head," Dr. Cohen told him.

I quickly called my single sister Hadassa, who lived nearby, to come and stay at my house for Shabbos. Luckily, I had already prepared all the Shabbos food on Thursday, and my house was ready for Shabbos. I foolishly decided that I didn't want to travel to Manhattan and risk being so far away from my children over Shabbos, so we headed towards the local emergency room instead.

As with most emergency rooms, I had to wait a couple of hours until I was seen. By then, it was already late Friday afternoon, and the MRI and CT departments were closed for the weekend. The doctor who examined me declared that I was fine and sent me home.

It was already Shabbos when I was discharged, so my husband's non-Jewish worker drove us home. On the way, we passed the *shul* where Dr. Cohen *davened,* and my husband went in to tell him what had occurred. He didn't seem too happy with the developments. "If your wife gets even slightly worse over Shabbos, call *Hatzolah* and go immediately to Beth Israel Hospital in Manhattan," he said grimly. "She might be in grave danger!"

I didn't think I was in danger because I was convinced that I had MS. A close family friend suffered from severe chronic progressive Multiple Sclerosis, and my symptoms were similar to all his early symptoms. He was extremely disabled by this time, and all I could think about was a future like his. I was terribly frightened.

Over Shabbos, I realized that my symptoms were primarily on my left side. "Okay, I probably have a brain tumor and not MS," I calmed myself. "It will be removed and I'll be just fine."

Though my symptoms intensified over Shabbos, I was in denial and did not tell my husband. I did not want to go to the hospital on Shabbos. In retrospect, I realize that my behavior was unwise and dangerous. In such life threatening situations, *halachah* not only permits, but demands, that one seek immediate medical attention. Perhaps things would have been a bit easier later on had I had followed the advice of Dr. Cohen.

On *Motzei Shabbos*, we called Dr. Cohen again. He told us to go to Beth Israel Hospital in Manhattan right away and insist on an MRI. Hadassa babysat once again, and we left immediately. Just like Friday, the wait was several hours long. We sat there watching all the weekend drunks being brought in. They were all seen right away, but I had to wait patiently for quite some time.

Finally after midnight, my name was called. Since I seemed fine outwardly, the ER doctor did not know what to do with me. While we were consulting with him, my vision became double, and he realized something was seriously wrong. An MRI could not be performed, since the department was closed, so he ordered a CT scan instead.

I waited a full hour, until three a.m., for the CT scan. Afterwards, I was brought to a cubicle to wait some more. A few minutes later, a nurse came in and gave me a hospital

Precarious Diagnosis

gown to change into and a bag for my belongings. Then, she put me on a gurney and started an IV. I still didn't know what was wrong with me, but I was too exhausted to ask questions and relieved to finally be able to lie down.

Later, when my husband walked in after consulting with the doctors, I immediately asked, "Do I have MS?" It was my only concern at the time.

"No you don't," he told me.

"Are you sure?"

"Yes," he reassured me.

"*Boruch Hashem!*" I exclaimed. Though I didn't know how serious my condition was, I was just thrilled to know that I didn't have MS.

The attending doctor explained that they had found bleeding in my brain stem, and though the CT scan did not show enough for a diagnosis, it was clear that I was in an emergency situation. Dr. Schick had already been contacted, and the doctor was ordered to admit me and immediately begin administering Decadron, a steroid medication, to stop inflammation.

My husband had to deal with the frightening news alone, since he did not want to distress me by telling me the whole truth. I was wheeled to the neurological step-down unit while my husband drove home to my children, hoping to catch a few hours of sleep before dawn.

On Sunday morning, my husband returned to spend the day with me. In the early afternoon, I had an MRI. They found a cavernous angioma, that was hemorrhaging in my brainstem, as well as traces of two previous small hemorrhages, which had caused the tingling sensation I had felt on my lip twice before. I was actively hemorrhaging and had I not been put on Decadron the night before, the bleed could have been fatal.

I had never heard of a cavernous angioma, which is also referred to as a cerebral cavernous malformation (CCM). The doctor explained that this is a collection of small blood vessels in the central nervous system that are enlarged and malformed, like an internal raspberry birthmark. This is a defect that some people are born with, and they can sometimes live their entire lives without ever being aware of its presence. When people die suddenly of an aneurysm, this is one of the possible causes, as a CCM hemorrhage can sometimes be immediately fatal. In my case, the hemorrhaging had caused inflammation to the area, resulting in neurological deficits.

I continued receiving an IV drip of Decadron throughout my stay at the hospital. Though I didn't actually feel ill, I was extremely uncoordinated, and I suffered from annoying double vision. Though Dr. Schick explained the gravity of my situation to my husband, he didn't give me too much information, and I wasn't particularly worried. I spent my days in boredom, sometimes relieving the monotony by speaking on the telephone.

Meanwhile, my sister Hadassa had moved into my house to take care of my children. During the day, when she was at work, they spent the time at Zehava Pearl's house.

Precarious Diagnosis

One day, while I was in Beth Israel, a neurologist with a group of about six students came into my room. The doctor explained my condition to his students and in front of me declared, "There is nothing that can be done for this patient."

My husband, who was there at the time, asked the neurologist for his business card. After the doctor walked out of the room, he told me, "When you are all better, we will go back to this *kofer* and show him that he has no right to write someone off like that. Hashem can do miracles."

Since my condition was stable and there was nothing else the hospital could do for me, I was discharged on Thursday morning. Before I left, Dr. Schick ordered me to refrain from any lifting or strenuous activity, since that could cause more hemorrhaging. He also prescribed Decadron, which I would continue taking orally at home.

Thus, I was soon heading back home with my husband. Though I was eager to see my children again, we were both in a pensive mood as we approached Monsey. We knew there were difficult days ahead, and we were filled with trepidation as we wondered what the future would bring.

2
In Limbo

Though the recent turn of events had taken me by complete surprise, I must admit that I was no stranger to adversity. My family had encountered various challenges when I was growing up, and I had learned to be strong and independent when I was still quite young. In fact, I was the backbone of the family; everyone turned to me for guidance and advice, and it was I who arranged most of the family gatherings. Moreover, since my parents live close to two hours away and my in-laws live overseas in England, I realized immediately that my husband and I would have minimal support as we faced the challenges that awaited us.

Our next step was to determine how to proceed with my treatment. Dr. Schick had explained that, over the course of several months, the blood would be reabsorbed, and my symptoms would disappear. Nonetheless, since the cavernous angioma had already bled three times, I was at great risk of hemorrhaging again. Another such incident, he warned us, could very well be fatal. Thus, he advised us to begin looking immediately for a neurosurgeon that would be willing to remove it.

Unfortunately, this was not as simple as one would think, since not one local neurosurgeon was willing to operate. My husband went from one neurosurgeon to another in Manhattan, and they all claimed that because of the sensitive location of the malformation, the mass could not be removed. My husband stubbornly refused to accept that answer, and with the help of Dr. Schick, he continued searching for a doctor who would perform the risky surgery. Eventually, he was put in touch with Dr. Robert F. Spetzler, a world-renowned neurosurgeon of the Barrow Neurological Institute in Phoenix, Arizona, who agreed to consider taking my case.

At around this time, my husband and I finally informed my parents and in-laws of my situation. Since we had not wanted to alarm them, we kept my condition a secret until we had a definite diagnosis and plan of action. Once the word was out, numerous family members called to inquire about my wellbeing and voice their concern.

Meanwhile, I continued taking Decadron every day. While the drug has lifesaving abilities, it also causes numerous side effects, including numbing one's emotions and distorting the thinking process. Thus to everyone's surprise, I appeared to be rather apathetic to my medical condition, and I discussed it in a nonchalant, detached manner.

Other side effects of the steroids included bloating, an increased appetite, and severe insomnia. I slept an average of three or four hours a night, and though I tried numerous sleeping pills, none were effective. I also felt moody and depressed, and I cried frequently. What distressed me most during this period was not my medical condition, but my physical dysfunction.

My husband hired a Columbian woman named Beatrice as a nanny and housekeeper, since I was unable to care for my children or home. Beatrice was a pleasant, petite woman who was about forty years old. She lived with us all week and went home for the weekends. Over Shabbos, when she wasn't there, Hadassa managed the house and took care of my children.

Since I was also unable to prepare meals, my friend Ruchala arranged for different people to cook supper for us every night. It was delivered at around five o'clock. By that time I was always so exhausted that I could barely move.

After eating, I awkwardly dragged myself up the stairs to get ready for bed. I would take a shower and then sit on my rocking chair for twenty minutes to regain enough strength to finish preparing for bed. Afterward, I would fall into bed in exhaustion, but to my frustration, I would just lie there, unable to fall asleep.

Beatrice was wonderful with my children, and after only a few days, Shloimy preferred her to me. Though I was grateful that he felt so comfortable with her, I felt saddened that my own child did not want me. Besides, I missed nursing him terribly. However, I thanked Hashem that he was such a good baby and had adjusted to formula so easily. At night, Beatrice slept in his room and gave him a bottle when he cried.

I awoke each morning before six and could not fall asleep again. At around six thirty, when I heard Shloimy wake up, I would go into his room. I was happy to have some company after a long, sleepless night. Libby usually woke up shortly thereafter. I would take her out of her crib and struggle to diaper her. Then we all headed downstairs, where I prepared Shloimy's breakfast cereal. Since I was too uncoordinated to feed him myself, Beatrice fed him while I ate my breakfast.

After breakfast, I began my long day of doing nothing. I was terribly bored and couldn't do much. I felt depressed from the steroid medication, and the fact that I was so dysfunctional only aggravated the situation. I couldn't drive and didn't leave the house. Though Beatrice could drive, my husband did not want her to take me out; he was afraid that any exertion would cause me to hemorrhage again.

Sitting at home, I had no way to fill my time. There was so little I could do. My balance was impaired, and I had to sit on the edge of my bed when I got dressed. When I poured a drink, some always missed the cup and spilled. Whenever I tried feeding my children, I ended up making a mess. I felt useless and cried all the time out of helplessness and frustration.

Shortly after I came home from the hospital, I realized that Libby's shoes were too small. I asked my brother Yaakov to drive us to the shoe store. When I walked inside, I couldn't focus long enough to choose a new pair, so I simply asked the salesman to give me the next size of the shoes that she was wearing.

In Limbo

For about a month, I was in limbo, sitting at home without a clear plan for the future. When I returned to Dr. Schick for a follow-up checkup, he saw that I had become weaker and less coordinated. He sent me for another MRI to see what was happening. The MRI showed that the bleeding had stopped, but somehow I was still becoming weaker. Dr. Schick recommended that I have surgery as soon as possible.

Usually patients in my condition are told to wait until their blood is reabsorbed. This way, there is no extra blood at the surgical site, and it's less complicated for the surgeon to see what he is doing. Also, the recovery tends to be significantly quicker, when the patient starts off with less inflammation. In my case though, Dr. Schick was concerned that it was too dangerous for me to delay the surgery.

Meanwhile, my medical records had been forwarded to Dr. Spetzler in Arizona, and after reviewing them, he informed us that he was willing to operate.

During this entire time, my husband consulted regularly with his mentor, Rabbi Hartman. Rabbi Hartman was a close confidant of the Steipler, *zt"l,* and the Satmar Rebbe, *zt"l,* and though he is a great *talmid chacham* and true *gadol,* he humbly prefers to remain out of the limelight.

At this time my husband contacted Rabbi Hartman again to update him about Dr. Spetzler's positive response. He strongly encouraged us to go ahead with the surgery as soon as possible, but advised us to first get a clear *brochah* from Rav Chaim Kanievsky.

My husband's brother, who lives in Bnei Brak, went to Rav Chaim Kanievsky on our behalf. Rav Kanievsky took my name, and listened closely to the whole story. After inquiring about some additional details, Rav Kanievsky declared that not only is it advisable for me to have surgery, but "it is a *mitzvah* for her to go *gleich, gleich, un zi vet huben ah refuah shleimah ingantzen.*" (She should go immediately, immediately, and she will have a complete and total recovery.)

Rav Kanievsky's blessing for a complete recovery was just what we had hoped to hear. Thus, with his reassuring words in mind, we scheduled my surgery for February 13, 2006, and booked tickets to Arizona.

3
Arizona

My flight was scheduled for early Sunday morning, February 12, 2006. The weather forecast predicted about two feet of snow, which was supposed to start falling shortly after midnight. My husband called the airline to see if there were any earlier available flights, but there weren't any. We decided to go to the airport and hope for the best.

I said a tearful good night to my children, thinking I would be away for about a week. The snow had already begun falling heavily when we left for the airport at around two a.m. My husband had a four-wheel drive vehicle, so he had no difficulty maneuvering it over the slippery roads. The highways were almost completely deserted, as few dared to leave their homes that night.

When we arrived at the airport, we headed directly to the check-in counter.

"I'm sorry," an agent told us, "all flights are delayed."

Though we were able to check in our luggage, we spent all of Sunday sitting in the airport and watching the snow fall. With each passing hour, we became even more anxious, since I was scheduled to register at the hospital in Arizona and have another MRI that same afternoon.

Throughout the day, there were repeated announcements about canceled flights. The snow finally stopped falling sometime in the afternoon, but the announcements for delays continued. Then, when the runways were at last cleared for takeoff, we learned that our flight had been canceled. FAA regulations prohibit pilots from flying after they have been awake for more than a certain amount of time. Since our pilots had been on duty for so long, they could no longer fly.

As airline personnel became busy re-booking flights for all passengers, my husband desperately explained our situation. "I'm sorry," an airline representative told him, "but there are no available seats on any flight to your destination until Wednesday. There is nothing we can do for you."

We were at a loss. It was crucial that we get to Arizona immediately, but even after trying other airlines, we could not find an available flight. Finally, my husband demanded to speak to a supervisor at the check-in counter. She was very sympathetic to our plight and told us to come back early the following morning as standby. "I will try my best to help you," she promised.

We did not want to make the one and a half hour drive back home, especially since we would have to turn right back before long. Desperate for some sleep, we tried to find a local hotel for the night, but due to the flight cancellations, all the rooms within a fifty-mile radius were completely booked. We were exhausted from not having slept the night before and having spent the entire day waiting in the airport.

My husband decided to call a friend, who lived fifteen minutes away from the airport. Fortunately, he immediately agreed to help us. He sent someone to pick us up. They served us supper and put us up for the night. The man's wife thoughtfully washed the clothes I had been wearing, and after a refreshing shower, I fell into bed exhausted. My insomnia kept me awake most of the night; nevertheless a comfortable bed was rejuvenating.

After a few hours' rest, we were back at the airport at the crack of dawn. When we arrived there, we realized that we had been fortunate that our flight had been cancelled. After we had left, a plane had skidded on the runway, causing all waiting planes to turn back. Thus, hundreds of people from all uncancelled flights were left stranded with only their carry-on luggage, and they had camped out on the airport floor overnight. We were glad that, while we hadn't made it to our destination either, at least we had had a decent night's rest.

When we reached the check-in counter, we were not given boarding passes or assigned seats, but were told to wait at the gate. Once the flight would be fully boarded, our names would be called if there were any available seats. We sat in the waiting area saying *tehillim* and *davening* that we would be able to board the flight.

Finally, our prayers were answered, and we heard our names being announced. The kind supervisor had somehow arranged seats for us on the flight.

The flight to Arizona lasted six hours. I did not get a seat next to my husband, but I was so grateful to be on the plane, that I didn't mind. During the flight I felt odd, as if I was an observer to my situation. I watched the unfolding events in a detached manner, devoid of emotion. I didn't even miss my children, and it bothered me that I felt that way.

We arrived in Arizona on Monday afternoon. We went from a cold winter blizzard to the beautiful warm sunshine of Arizona. I had no time to enjoy the beautiful weather though, since I had to rush to register at the hospital, see Doctor Spetzler in his office, and have an MRI that afternoon. The MRI would create a computer image of my brain which would assist the doctor with my surgery. My surgery was rescheduled for the following morning. Finally, after our hectic afternoon, we checked into a hotel and ate supper from the supply of food that my husband had packed.

We arrived at the hospital at seven the next morning. I went into surgery naively optimistic, unaware of what the aftereffects would be. Of course, the doctor had warned me. "The surgery will be like another hemorrhage, and the symptoms will be considerably worse afterwards," he had told me.

Nonetheless, I didn't realize the full extent of how significantly worse it could possibly be. My mind was also clouded from the effects of the steroids, and I was feeling indifferent to all the details of my illness. "Okay, I'll be a bit clumsier," I figured, "my double vision will worsen, and I'll feel a little number. How much worse can it get?"

I was in for the shock of my life!

After eight hours of surgery, I awoke in a fog. The doctor was squeezing my big toe and calling my name. My husband gave me the news that my sister in-law in Israel had given birth to a baby girl during the operation. Then I slipped back into oblivion.

When I awoke again, I realized I was almost completely numb on my entire left side, from my toes all the way up to my forehead, and I couldn't move anything at all. They had put Vaseline in my eyes to keep them moist during surgery, and my vision was double and blurred. I could see almost nothing. My speech was terribly slurred; my voice was deeper than usual, and I could only speak in a monotone. On top of all that, I felt rapid spinning in my head, which was extremely distressing.

I was horrified and in complete shock. I had not expected anything of the sort. The doctor, on the other hand, was thrilled with the outcome of the surgery. "The surgery went exceptionally well, without any complications," he told my husband. "Your wife is extremely lucky. The fact that she is breathing on her own, is a miracle."

But I didn't feel lucky at all! All the comforting words in the world could not make me feel better, and I could not stop crying.

The surgery had been performed through a very small incision behind my right ear, and there was now a tube running from the site of my surgery down my spine, draining excess fluid through a hole in my lower back. I was in the ICU and had to be carefully monitored to keep the pressure in my brain just right. Each time I adjusted the bed up or down, the nurse had to readjust the drain.

I don't remember this, but my husband has told me that, because I was so uncomfortable, I kept moving my bed up and down every few minutes. Each time I moved, an alarm sounded, and the nurse had to readjust the drain. "It just drove her crazy," he said.

Every few hours, a nurse would approach my bedside and ask, "What's your name?"

"Rivkah Zucker," I'd reply.

"Where are you?"

"At the BNI in Saint Joseph's Hospital."

"Who is the president?"

"George Bush," I'd answer.

"What's today's date?"

And so on and so on. These questions were annoying, but they had to make sure I remained cognitive. Any confusion could be a sign of a problem.

The doctor ordered a post-op MRI and saw that my surgery had gone well. Now I had to be kept infection-free and weaned off the steroids. My blood pressure was exceedingly high, which was another side affect of Decadron, and I was put on a blood pressure medication to lower it.

Arizona

I stayed in the ICU until Friday, when they finally removed the drain from my spine. Afterwards, I was given my own room, where I stayed until Wednesday evening.

I have little memory of my stay in Arizona, which in reality is a good thing. I know I was miserable, depressed, scared and frustrated. I felt awful: I cried a lot, I could barely speak, and I was awfully lonely.

My husband discussed my options for rehabilitation with the doctors. Since I live in Rockland County, New York, and wanted to be close to home, they recommended the Scenic View Hospital, which is a rehab center located about twenty five minutes from my home. My husband arranged for me to be admitted there on Thursday morning, and he booked tickets for us to fly back on Wednesday evening.

I went to the airport by ambulette on a stretcher and flew home first class. Unlike a luxury first class seat on an international flight, it was just slightly larger than economy class and located at the front of the plane.

Getting me to my seat was no easy feat. I was strapped onto a special narrow wheelchair without armrests and then transferred to my seat. I slept through most of the flight and don't remember much about it. I only know I was excited to be heading back to New York, though I did not realize just how many months would pass before I would actually see my home again.

My husband remembers:

In the weeks following Rivkah's diagnosis, she was the eye of the storm. She stayed at home, trying her best to cope, while I began running around to find a doctor who would operate on her. Because her condition was so volatile, I tried my best to protect her. She didn't realize how critical her situation was, and she was not aware of all the difficulties related to finding a doctor and dealing with our insurance.

For the first few weeks, I hardly slept more than a couple of hours each night. I spent hours speaking to insurance representatives and scheduling appointments with every major surgeon in Manhattan. It was a real nightmare dealing with aloof office staff of world-class surgeons, the parking situation in Manhattan as I ran from place to place, and the unsympathetic insurance representatives. I consulted countless times with my mentor, Rabbi Hartman, who was a constant source of strength and encouragement. I did not make any decision without discussing it with him first.

It is difficult to describe my relief when we heard at last that Dr. Spetzler was willing to operate. After our eventful journey to Arizona, we met him for the first time in his office. I was immediately impressed by his compassionate and humble demeanor. His attitude was reflected throughout the establishment, and all the employees, from the nurses to the janitors, were proud of the place and conscious of their role in helping to make it an outstanding institution.

During our initial meeting, my wife asked Dr. Spetzler how long he thought the surgery would take.

"I can't say," he replied. "Usually around seven or eight hours. I work and G-d does the rest."

That was all I needed to hear to put my heart at ease. I knew that, be'ezras Hashem, we had found the right shaliach to heal Rivkah.

During the operation, I did not feel anxious or scared. I knew that we were doing the right thing in going ahead with the risky but necessary operation, and I felt confident, since we had received a gadol's havtachah. Rav Chaim Kanievsky himself had assured my brother that all would be well.

At first, I went into the waiting room, which was filled with sobbing family members of other patients. I said some tehillim and learned my daily shiur on Rivkah's behalf. Then, I returned to my hotel room to catch up on some much-needed sleep. The operation was expected to last a number of hours, and I knew the best way to help Rivkah was to make sure that I would be well-rested for her afterwards.

In truth, my emotions never played a big role in the first months of our ordeal. I think that it was a blessing that I was so overwhelmed taking care of all the details involved in Rivkah's care. I never had a chance to sit down and really absorb the enormity of what was happening.

During the surgery itself, the words of Rabbi Hartman and Rav Kanievsky echoed in my mind reassuringly, again allaying my fears. The one time I did feel gripped by fear was when I saw Rivkah's condition in the first weeks after surgery. To say that she was not acting like herself would be a huge understatement, and for some time I was desperately afraid that I might never get my wife back.

4
Scenic View Rehab Center

I vaguely remember the ride from the airport to Scenic View Rehab Center. I was admitted to unit 4A, which is the Traumatic Brain Injury Unit. It is also an acute therapy ward, which meant I would be given three hours of therapy per day. I don't recall much of my first few weeks there. I do remember that I was extremely exhausted and miserable. Each day, I had two half-hour sessions of occupational therapy, two half-hour sessions of physical therapy, and two half-hour sessions of speech therapy.

I was assigned to a private room. My husband was able to sleep there with me and stay past visiting hours. The only drawback was that I felt extremely lonely and isolated. I am an extrovert and thrive on companionship. I love being surrounded by people, and in my state, I was not only alone, but also completely helpless. I was able to do almost nothing. I felt like a prisoner in my own body. I couldn't read due to my blurred and double vision, and I couldn't even hold a book or turn pages. Light bothered my eyes immensely, so I couldn't watch TV either. In fact, I couldn't tolerate any light at all. I kept the lights off in my room, and even then, I closed my eyes most of the time.

My room had a beautiful view facing the Hudson River, with mountains in the background. All my visitors admired the view, but I was unable to enjoy it in my condition. It irritated me how everyone commented on it cheerily.

My full name is Etta Rivkah, and all my legal and insurance documents bear my full name. In Arizona, after my surgery, all the doctors and nurses called me Etta, pronouncing it Edda. I had no energy or will to correct them, so I just learned to respond to Edda.

When I arrived at Scenic View Rehab Center, the same thing happened, and again I responded to "Edda." This went on for about a month, until I finally had enough oomph to say something. All the nurses had to relearn my name and start calling me Rivkah. It was hard on them at first, but they caught on eventually.

After I was in Scenic View Rehab Center for about two weeks, I realized that the steroids distorted my thinking and caused me great anxiety. I had come to Scenic View with precise instructions from Dr. Spetzler, outlining the exact regiment of how my steroids should be decreased. The side effects were disturbing me greatly, and I was not in a very rational state of mind. I begged the doctor to lower my dose more quickly. The neurologist at Scenic View listened to my pleas and lowered my steroid dosage without following the specific instructions of Dr. Spetzler.

Scenic View Rehab Center

A few days afterwards, my husband spent Shabbos with me, and he noticed a deterioration of my right side coordination. He became quite concerned. I could barely use my right hand. I couldn't even grasp cut up pieces of fruit. I also felt a slight numbness on the right side of my face. My husband spoke to the nurse in charge, and she called the house doctor who was overseeing the entire hospital for the weekend. The doctor, who came to see me, was named Dr. Mohammad; he came to my bedside wearing a turban, beard, and long robe. I greeted him amicably and tried to explain what was wrong. He turned to my husband and said, "Nothing is wrong with your wife. She is smiling."

As soon as Shabbos was over, my husband called Dr. Schick on his emergency number. Dr. Schick instructed my husband to take me to Beth Israel hospital for another MRI of my brain. He also arranged for a bed for me, but I adamantly refused to go to Beth Israel. A visit there would require me to travel by ambulance for about an hour and a half, and I didn't think I would be able to handle it.

Instead of going to Manhattan, I went by ambulance to a local emergency room, about twenty five-minutes away, for a CT scan. My husband followed in his pick-up truck. I had to wait for about an hour until they were able to see me, and another hour for the results, which *boruch* Hashem came back all clear.

Once we had the results, I had to wait close to two hours to be discharged. I was lying on a gurney under bright lights in a curtained off section of the emergency room. I just kept my eyes closed and tried to block everything out. I was extremely uncomfortable. The bright lights greatly disturbed me, and I also had to use the bathroom urgently.

Frustrated at being unable to help me, my husband decided to wheel me out, put the stretcher in the back of his closed pick-up truck, and drive me back to Scenic View. He had it all figured out, how he would secure the stretcher in the bed of his truck. Although I didn't agree to his idea, I was not in a condition to voice my opinion. When the nurses saw my husband begin to wheel me out, they called the police. The police wanted to arrest him, but agreed in the end to make my husband stay outside with the security guard watching. I was left alone, unable to fend for myself, and when I called out to the nurses, they just ignored me.

Finally, a nurse came, and I asked her what was going on. Because my speech was so slurred and unintelligible, they all thought I was crazy and treated me in a condescending manner. "The doctor who needs to sign you out is busy with a code patient, who is in cardiopulmonary arrest," she told me brusquely.

I was so uncomfortable, frustrated and exhausted. The steroids caused me to be uninhibited. I would just blurt out whatever was on my mind, sometimes saying things that were completely out of character or inappropriate. Now, upset at the staff's indifference, I exclaimed, "I hope he dies quickly!"

The nurse was furious and stormed out. Finally, after what felt like hours later, she returned. "I am truly sorry," I told her. "I meant to say, 'I hope the doctor revives him quickly.'"

She accepted that, but it was still a while until I was discharged. The same medics, who brought me in hours earlier, had just brought in another patient, so they took me back to Scenic View at about five o'clock in the morning. It was a long, harrowing night and I was exhausted. I never thought I would be so happy to be back in Scenic View, in my own hospital bed with all the familiar nurses and surroundings.

The doctors eventually figured out that my symptoms were caused by swelling in the brain due to withdrawal from the steroids. They had to raise my dosage again. I wasn't pleased, but I was in danger of permanent brain damage. I realized that the doctor had made an error in judegement when he yielded to my request without following the instructions of Dr. Spetzler.

Though I don't remember this too clearly, my husband has told me that immediately after the surgery my left side was completely useless, but my right hand was fully functional. I vaguely remember dialing on my cell phone, eating ice cream from a cone, adjusting my bed without difficulty and feeding myself. After my steroids dosage was lowered too quickly, I was barely able to use my right hand, and it was a long and slow recovery.

A few days after this incident, I was sitting alone in my room in the wheelchair, when my lunch tray was delivered. Since I couldn't move my left side, and I'd lost most of my right side's use, I couldn't open the food or eat anything by myself. Nonetheless, I wanted to move the tray a couple of inches towards me. My sudden, uncontrolled movement jerked the tray, causing a hot cup of water to tip over. The scorching water spilled all over my left thigh.

My voice was so weak at the time that I couldn't even yell. The call bell was only a few feet away from me, but I was unable to propel my wheelchair yet. Somehow I managed to drag myself over to press it. It felt like eternity until someone finally responded. I was sitting in the boiling water the whole time. When a nurse finally came, she stripped off my clothes and put me into bed. It took two aides to transfer me into bed then. They photographed and measured the burn. It was 15x20 centimeters. The nurses put cream on it and bandaged me up.

I remember calling my husband on the telephone and crying hysterically. I was most upset about being so dysfunctional and causing this to myself. The burn was on my left side, which had diminished sensation, so it was not as painful as it would have been under normal circumstances.

The hospital called in a plastic surgeon for consultation. Due to the severity of my burn, he recommended skin grafting. Since I was on steroids, I was not a candidate for surgery at the time. The steroids also caused me to feel apathetic, and I was truly indifferent about the matter. Since the burn wrapped around under my thigh, sitting or lying on it would cause pressure to the area. The doctor ordered an anti-pressure mattress for me, so that it could heal properly. He also recommended that I not sit up in the wheelchair for more than two hours at a time. I was pleased with the doctor's orders. I couldn't tolerate sitting up for long periods, and the burn provided a good excuse for staying in bed.

Scenic View Rehab Center

The anti-pressure mattress was also beneficial, since I could barely move around on my own and it prevented bedsores.

A few days after I was burned, the neurologist, who was the main doctor on the unit, wanted to examine the burn. He walked into my room with a cup of hot coffee in his hand and approached my bed. I eyed the steaming cup in horror.

"Please don't come close to me with that," I said.

At first, the doctor thought that I was trying to be funny, but I was serious. I felt that it was irresponsible, and considering the situation, even insensitive, for a doctor to approach a patient's bedside with a scalding drink in his hand!

After I was burned, the head nurse would not allow me to have any meals in my room unless I had someone with me. Even though I no longer received hot water, and I was unable to open my food by myself, she ordered all my meals to be delivered to the nurses' desk. All the nurse's aides were too busy to help me in the morning, so they wheeled me out to sit by the nurses' station. A nurse would set up my breakfast in front of me on a tray table and then leave me to eat on my own. I was extremely uncoordinated and created a big mess. It was awfully embarrassing to eat in public in my state.

During lunch, the head nurse insisted I eat in the dining room with all the other patients. Most patients ate in the dining room, and there were two nurse's aides overseeing and assisting everyone. A nurse's aide wheeled me into the dining room, put a plastic bib on me and opened my lunch. I had a prepackaged kosher meal of meatballs and spaghetti, which I couldn't eat by myself. When I asked the aide to help me, she said, "I have many others to help. I can't sit with you the whole time."

I ate about two bites and then asked to be brought back to my room. My head was spinning, and the bright lights in the dining room were unbearable. Though I was quite hungry, I didn't see the point of staying there, since I couldn't feed myself properly anyways. After that incident, I refused to go back to the dining room.

That same day, I had a visitor, my good friend Sarah Rosemann. I told her that I couldn't feed myself and the nurses refused to help me. She was very upset when she heard this. "I'll arrange for people to come feed you," she promised.

At the time, I was also experiencing a lot of anxiety. I tried to figure out what would help me feel better. Aside from the fact that the steroids were wreaking havoc on my moods, I realized I was lonely and needed company. I concluded that if I would have visitors during all my waking moments, I would feel less lonesome and more secure. Thus, two dear friends, Zehava Pearl and Sarah Rosemann, came to my rescue. These kind, compassionate women organized visitors for me from seven thirty in the morning until nine in the evening, when visiting hours were over. My visitors kept me company and fed me my meals for as long as I was unable to do so.

I eagerly anticipated the new change in my routine. I knew that with my visitors, my special angels of mercy, life was bound to get better.

5
Total Dysfunction

*I*n the weeks following my surgery, I was in a constant state of anguish. I felt imprisoned by my dysfunctional body and extremely vulnerable. I was as helpless as a newborn infant, and as a formerly independent adult, the situation was extremely distressing. Words can't adequately portray the extent of my pain, but I will try and provide a glimpse of what I went through.

Whenever I was in an upright position, the spinning in my head increased. Dr. Spetzler said that the more I sat up, the sooner the sensation would go away; however, I couldn't tolerate sitting. It was torturous. As much as I wanted to sit upright and make the spinning go away, I kept giving up and spent most of my time lying in bed. I tried to sleep with my head upright. I hoped that that would help the spinning go away sooner, but there was absolutely no relief. When my eyes were closed, I still felt the spinning. Even during the times when I did not feel the sensation, it resumed upon the slightest exertion.

One of the steriods' side effects was increased sweating. I always felt hot and sweaty, and my palms were constantly wet. I was extremely uncomfortable and could find no relief. My room was hot, dry and stuffy, and the windows were screwed shut. My husband brought a humidifier, but it didn't help. My lips were always chapped, but ChapStick and Vaseline made little difference. My cousin advised me to ask the nurses for a bag of ice, and that did cool me a bit, as I would place it on different parts of myself. I slept with only a thin sheet at night, and even that was more than I needed at times.

I was uncomfortable in whatever position I was in. I felt lopsided due to the numbness on my left side. When I was sitting up in the wheelchair, it felt like my left foot was going right through the floor. If I was in bed, my left knee felt like it was bent, and my leg was protruding through my mattress. I would have the sensation that my left hand was in one position, but when I looked at it, I saw it was in a completely different position altogether. My left arm and hand were kept elevated on a pillow to prevent swelling. Poor circulation caused my left foot and hand to feel cold all the time.

The muscles on my left side started to atrophy, and my left hand became so thin that my palm and wrist were about the same width. A friend brought me a red string from Israel and put it on my left wrist. It slipped off and vanished the next day.

I could not sit up without support. Unless I was holding onto something, I would just topple over, like an infant who cannot sit up yet. Scenic View provided me with a wheelchair that had a high back and sides that curved in to help me stay upright. My left side was so weak, that even with a special chair I usually leaned to the right. Due to the numbness, I felt lopsided even when I was sitting straight, and I would constantly ask people to tell me how I was sitting. My physical therapist told me to sit in front of the mirror and pay attention to how it felt when I was sitting straight.

I was never comfortable; when I was in bed, I thought I would feel better sitting in the chair, and when I was in the chair; I wanted to be in bed. Sometimes I asked the nurse to take me to the bathroom, just so I could change positions. My coccyx was constantly in pain, and there was nothing I could do to find relief. I was belted into the wheelchair, and the seatbelt was closed from behind. If I slid a bit forward, I was unable to readjust myself. I felt miserable.

I had severe insomnia and spent many hours each night awake in bed. I was given sleeping pills, but they weren't effective. The steroids caused all kinds of strange thoughts and intense anxiety, so I spent hours pondering and worrying about things that did not even make sense. I first went to sleep without a sleeping pill and slept for about four hours. When I awoke, I would be unable to fall back asleep, so I'd ring the nurse for my medication. I hoped if I would take it later in the night, I might sleep later in the morning. However, even then, I would still wake up around five thirty every morning and just lie in bed with my mind in motion.

One time I woke up at around three a.m. and could not fall back asleep. I pressed the call bell to request a sleeping pill, but no one came. I pressed the bell again and again. After a while I realized that my call bell was broken. I started calling out for a nurse to come to my room. My room was far away from the nurse's station, and my voice was weak, so no one heard me.

I was alone in the room, unable to do anything for myself. I felt anxious and terrified, and my mind filled with all kinds of frightening and ridiculous thoughts. After a while, I realized that my cell phone was within my reach. Somehow, I managed to call my husband. I was crying so hysterically, I could barely explain what was wrong. My husband called the nurses' station and someone came to me right away. It was a frightening experience. Under normal circumstances, I would not have panicked, but in my condition, it made me realize just how helpless I truly was.

After that incident, I made sure to have my cell phone in my bed every night except for Shabbos, when someone usually slept in my room with me. I had a difficult time with the telephone altogether. My cell phone was a flip phone, and I could not open it or dial properly. Someone suggested that I open it with my teeth. Although I was able to answer it when it rang, I didn't have the strength to hold it up to my ear. Because of its small size, I also found it difficult to grasp. I had to make sure to ask someone to charge it for me, since I could not do that by myself.

Many times when I answered the phone by opening it with my teeth, it would snap shut right away. This was quite frustrating. Eventually, my cell phone disappeared, and I assumed that it had been stolen. It had been hard to handle, and in truth I didn't miss it. The hospital phone was easier for me to grasp, but it was too heavy and cumbersome. I had the nurse place it in my bed each night, so that I'd have it within reach.

Talking while holding the phone to my ear was difficult for me. It was too taxing to talk on the phone while I was sitting up, so I kept conversations short. When I was in bed, it was much easier, since I was able to prop the phone between my pillow and shoulder. I was only able to make local calls with the hospital phone, but the dexterity in my right hand was so poor that I could not dial accurately. I'd hold the phone and dial with my thumb, but I would constantly hit the wrong button and have to start all over again. I finally thought of simply dialing zero and asking the operator to connect me. Even then, I still did not always manage to hit the correct button on the first try.

After I was in Scenic View for about two weeks, I started feeling the sensation of pins and needles running up and down the whole left side of my body. At the same time, I started having anxiety attacks. I would start sweating, my heart would race and pound in my chest, and I felt as though I was going to faint. Between the pins and needles and the anxiety, I was in an almost constant state of panic. When I had an attack during my therapy sessions, I couldn't continue. I would have to be helped into bed and given a tranquilizer. The tranquilizer usually knocked me out, but, at the time, that was just fine with me.

When I first came to Scenic View, I still had the Foley catheter in from the surgery, and it was removed immediately after I arrived. My bladder muscles hadn't been working for over two weeks, so they forgot what to do. My bladder would fill up, and I just could not empty it as hard as I tried. The nurses used an ultrasound device to measure how full my bladder was, and when it reached a certain amount, they would empty it for me with a onetime use catheter.

Coordinating my schedule was tricky. I had to be in bed twice a day when the nurses dressed my burn and every four to six hours when they emptied my bladder. According to the plastic surgeon's orders, I wasn't supposed to be sitting in the wheelchair for more than two hours at a time. My therapy sessions took place in the therapy room, where I had to be up in the wheelchair. Though I am punctual by nature, it was impossible for me to always be on schedule. It was stressful that timing was out of my control, and I could not always get to my therapy sessions on time. I also developed a bladder infection and had to be on antibiotics for ten days, which just added to my troubles.

About a month into rehab, I developed a cold and my nose kept running. To my utter frustration, I couldn't even blow my nose properly. It was a challenge to pick up a tissue and keep it in a good position with one inept hand. After many tries, I eventually learned how to do it. However, when someone handed me a tissue, I wasn't able to position it correctly. I had to take it out of the box myself and hold it a certain way for it to work. I also was unable to use a tissue more than once, since I could not position the unused part of the tissue right. I used up loads and loads of tissues. Thankfully, a thoughtful friend brought me some soft tissues. The ones from the hospital were like sandpaper.

Despite all these difficulties, there were some improvements early on that gave me some hope. Most

Total Dysfunction

noteworthy is the sensation of finally "waking up" about two weeks after I arrived at Scenic View.

Although I was aware of my surroundings immediately after my surgery, I felt emotionally detached, as though I was merely an observer who was watching the events unfold. I observed things passively and felt uninterested in my care. If no one would have fed me, I would have just gone hungry. I had no will to do anything. I would just lie there and let others do things for me. I did not participate in getting dressed and did not care what I wore or ate. I performed the exercises the therapists instructed me to do, swallowed the pills the nurses gave me, and stuck out my arm when they needed to draw blood. I felt like a zombie, without any will of my own. I kept wondering, how I would recover if I didn't take a more active role in my therapy and overall care.

At one time, I tried to explain the active versus passive mode to my husband. I sounded so nonsensical that he thought that I was losing my mind. I also did not always think very lucidly. I was still on a heavy dose of Decadron, and the steroids clouded and distorted my thinking. It was like being in a dream state. When someone is dreaming, everything seems to make perfect sense, but once the person wakes up, the events do not make sense anymore. Even though I knew that my strange thoughts were caused by my medications, they drove me crazy. I would call my husband all the time and cry that the steroids were messing up my mind.

As I was weaned off the drug, the cloud lifted, and I was able to think more clearly and feel more normal. I suddenly felt that I wanted to get better. I wanted to participate in my therapy, and I started trying to move my left hand as often as possible.

In addition to my distorted thinking, the steroid medication, as well as the actual surgery, caused me to develop clinical depression. I could not have a conversation with anyone without crying in middle. As happens often after brain surgery, I would then start laughing uncontrollably. I was not in control of my emotions, and this was extremely disconcerting.

The hospital's resident psychiatrist prescribed the antidepressant Zoloft to help with my anxiety and take the edge off my depression. After taking it for just a couple of days, the anxiety went away. I still cried a lot, but not as much as before. My uncontrolled laughing ceased, and I finally felt more normal.

I was pleased when the doctor told me Zoloft is an antidepressant that can be stopped suddenly and is not addictive. For most others the dose must be lessened gradually. I was happy to hear this, since I didn't want to have to be weaned off yet another drug.

Though Zoloft has several possible side effects, the only one I experienced was dry mouth. It was quite uncomfortable and drinking did not help. A neighbor who was visiting suggested that I suck on candies, and she offered to bring me some. Since I would not be able to unwrap them myself, she said that she would unwrap them for me.

True to her word, the next time she visited, she brought a few zip lock bags, each containing candies of a different flavor. Each bag had a zipper that slid back and forth, and

Total Dysfunction

I was able to open and close the bags myself using my teeth. My mouth wasn't actually dry; the drug just caused a sensation of dryness, so the candies did not help, but I enjoyed them nonetheless.

At around this time, I received a large manila envelope in the mail from Yeshiva Darchei Torah in Far Rockaway. I asked a nurse to open the envelope for me. Inside I found over twenty get-well cards that had been written by a class of young boys. The teacher included a note, explaining that she had heard about my situation and had decided to allow her students to practice their writing skills by creating the cards and learning about *bikkur cholim.*

Though I do not know the teacher or any of her students, I was truly touched by the collection of sweet, thoughtful cards. I read them again and again. They helped me realize just how much a written note means to someone who is ill. Phone calls can be taxing and difficult for a patient, and they often come at inconvenient times. On the other hand, a card written to express sympathy and wish someone a speedy recovery is always appreciated and can be a source of continuous *chizuk.*

Undeniably, I needed all the *chizuk* I could get. I asked someone to create inspirational signs for me on her computer, hoping that they would help me survive my ordeal. I had the following signs printed and hung directly in front of my bed, so I was able to see them at all times:

"*Ivdu es Hashem b'simcha.*" *(Serve Hashem with joy.)*

"*Yeshuas Hashem k'heref ayin*" *(Hashem's salvation comes in the blink of an eye.)*

"Shivisi Hashem linegdi tomid" (I place Hashem before me at all times)

"Boruch gozer umikayeim" (Blessed is He who decrees and fulfills)

I specifically chose this particular verse from *Boruch She'amar*, because early on in rehab, a visitor had shared a beautiful interpretation on it. She explained that the word *'mikayeim'* can also be interpreted as 'sustains'; Hashem makes a *g'zeirah,* and then sustains and gives a person the strength to withstand it. This concept created a deep impression on me, and I read the *pasuk* again and again.

I also had another sign of a quote that I had once seen and thought appropriate: "Mile by mile, it's a trial; yard by yard, it's hard; but inch by inch, it's a cinch."

On another sign I listed things I had to be grateful for:

I am able to hear.

I am able to breathe.

I am able to see.

I am able to think.

I am able to swallow.

I am improving the use of my left hand.

My children are young and won't remember any of this.

My children are well taken care of.

I have the most caring, understanding and devoted husband.

I would read these signs when I was feeling especially down. I made an effort to internalize these messages, and I gained much *chizuk* from them. I also needed constant reassurance from my husband. I repeatedly asked him, "Do you really think I'll get better?"

"Of course you will," he always answered. "We have a *gadol's havtachah.*"

Then I would begin to cry and say, "I want to be all better already. I'm supposed to be home taking care of my children."

"This is where you are supposed to be now," he would remind me. "This is what Hashem wants."

"I know, but it is so hard," I'd weep.

I imagined that I was making a difficult, strenuous trek up an immense mountain. While each step was a challenge, I felt that if I remained focused on the summit – my eventual recovery – I would be able to persevere and make the climb. And so, I trudged through each painful day, with an eye to the future and hope in my heart.

My friend Shani remembers:

Dear Rivkah,

We grew up in the same hometown, went through the same educational system and then worked together. With your outgoing personality and ready smile, you are the kind of person people want to be around. You are a doer with a cheerful disposition that allows us to really have a good time together.

After I married and began building a family, I davened so much harder for you to do the same. My joy knew no bounds, when you followed suit. With your wonderful husband and two young, adorable children, life was so beautiful and wonderful. Until...

You weren't feeling right, and strange things were happening to you. When you were diagnosed, I took it very hard. We had gone through a great deal together, and it was difficult to believe this was happening to you.

Having worked in the medical field, I made some phone calls and did some research in order to understand what you were going through. You in turn acted oblivious to the seriousness of your situation. I was informed and understood the risks and possible outcome of brainstem surgery. I kept quiet, davened and waited.

Nothing could have prepared me for the conversation we had after surgery. With trembling hands and a fluttering heart, I phoned Phoenix, Arizona, to speak to you, my friend who had survived brainstem surgery. When I said hello, the voice that replied seemed to belong to a stranger. "Rivkah, is that you?" I asked. "Yes," you answered. Each word was said with tremendous effort, in a deep, monotonous voice.

It was difficult for you to speak, especially on the phone. I kept updated through your husband and your children's caretakers.

I recall asking your husband how he was doing in all this. He replied, "I wish I could have back the Rivkah I once knew, the Rivkah I married."

Speaking to you on the phone was emotionally draining and difficult for me. It took everything out of me. After I hung up, I needed to speak to someone immediately, to give me chizuk. My nights were sleepless, and my days often found me in tears.

Steroids were wreaking havoc on your emotions. Your voice, strength and sentiments were robbed from you, as well as your wonderful personality. I had a longing to visit you in Scenic View. Your husband urged me to overcome my fear of driving through Manhattan and just come. Was it only my fear of driving through Manhattan, or was it the fear of facing reality and seeing you in the state you were in?

The visit to Scenic View was a positive experience. I went with a few friends; I could not do it alone. As we walked through the main entrance, the two receptionists looked at each other. They guessed whom we were visiting. "This Rivkah is so famous; everyone seems to know her," they exclaimed.

We went up to your room and crowded around your bed. I happened to stand in the perfect spot for you to be able to see me without straining. We schmoozed and laughed together. You were well-liked and well taken care of at the rehab center. I was seeing it all for myself. With tremendous bitachon in Hashem, a wonderful positive attitude and a devoted husband, you were on your way to recovery.

With your upbeat manner, constant prayer and a mindset that nothing stands in the way of Hashem, "the One who heals all flesh and is wondrous in His ways," we knew you would see the light at the end of the tunnel.

Shani

6
Life in 4A

Shabbosos

My husband stayed with me in Scenic View the first few Shabbosos and slept on the pullout couch in my room. He brought along a cooler on wheels with all the Shabbos provisions. He recited Kiddush, ate the *seudos* with me and fed me. I didn't have much energy, so I stayed in bed and dozed most of the day. By the third Shabbos, I felt stronger and wanted more company and entertainment. My husband, however, was utterly exhausted after a long, difficult week of juggling his various responsibilities. During the week, he had to deal with the hospital and all the other issues involving my care. In addition, he oversaw our children's care, as he continued to work full time. Thus, he spent the entire week running between Scenic View, our home and his office, while sleeping only for a few hours each night. Shabbos was the only time he had to regain his strength and fortify himself for another tough week ahead, and so he slept for a good part of the day.

After that Shabbos, we realized that it would be beneficial for both of us if we arranged to have other people stay with me for Shabbos. I would be distracted and entertained by my company, and he would be able to catch up on much-needed sleep and spend some time with our children.

During the weeks that followed, my husband would bring a cooler of Shabbos food each Friday afternoon. It contained the basic Shabbos food, as well as many extras, for my company and me. In the beginning, my most frequent Shabbos guests were my cousin Rivky and my sister Hadassa, who often brought along her friend Blimi. Before long, Hadassa and Blimi were my Shabbos guests on three out of every four Shabbosos.

Twice, my mother and my aunt spent Shabbos with me. They stayed in the sleeping quarters that the hospital provided for patients' family members who stayed overnight. Bikur Cholim had put up an *eiruv* so people could carry between the buildings on Shabbos. They set up the tray table in my room, trying to make it resemble a real Shabbos table. They sang *zemiros* and schmoozed with me. I truly enjoyed their company and almost forgot my problems or where I was.

Another Shabbos, my cousin came, and she brought some games for us to play. I had rarely played games when I was younger and had not played any in years. To my surprise, I actually enjoyed playing games with her. Afterwards, I asked my husband and a friend to bring some games that I could keep in my room to play with visitors.

Leaving My Room

For the first two months, I didn't leave my room except to go to my therapy sessions. The bright lights in the hallways bothered my eyes. I constantly felt the spinning in my head and became disoriented easily, and so I felt most secure in my room.

One time a visitor wanted to take me outside. I did not feel up to it and reluctantly agreed to go, but not too much time passed before I asked to be brought back inside. The sunlight was painfully strong for me, and I could not enjoy the nice view. I also disliked being bumped along the sidewalk in the wheelchair. True, I was miserable indoors, but when someone took me out, I just wanted to go back inside again.

My therapists encouraged me to go to and from therapy on my own by propelling the wheelchair with my feet. It was extremely difficult for me to accomplish this. I could not use my left foot at all, and my right foot was weak and uncoordinated. My physical therapist tried to teach me to turn the right wheel with my right hand, and use my right foot to steer and help move myself forward. Because my arm was still weak, this was too difficult as well. I also could not coordinate my arm and leg at the same time.

At the beginning my therapists came to my room to take me, and they brought me back after each session. Eventually, I started to propel my wheelchair by myself, but only with my right foot at first. When I regained some movement in my left leg I tried to use my left leg as well, but my right leg did most of the work. Once I started using my legs, the wheelchair's leg rests were in the way and had to be removed.

In addition to learning how to maneuver the wheelchair, I also had to learn my way around. The therapy room was around a corner and down the hall, but my spatial perception was impaired, and I could not see well either. I always felt disoriented and had a hard time finding my way back to my room. The hallway floors in the hospital were not all level. In some places there was a slight incline; I felt as though I was dragging the wheelchair up a hill, and it was more difficult to move forward. In other areas, I was going downhill and the wheelchair would roll forward easily. Often, I used the handrail down the center of each wall to pull myself along with my right hand.

When I was moving my wheelchair with my feet, it took so much energy that my left thumb would bend inward towards my palm. I was unable to unbend it, unless I did so with my right hand. I asked my therapist about it, and she explained that the muscle that keeps the thumb out was very weak, and as I recruited all my strength to move, the stronger muscle that curls the thumb took over.

For the first month and a half, I didn't speak to any other patients. I was in my own little bubble of misery, trying my best to cope. I am normally outgoing and sociable and love talking to people, but I had so little energy and felt awful.

After about six weeks, I started socializing and making friends. I sometimes sat near the nurse's station and kept other lonely people company. I still spent most of my time in my room, but my gloom was starting to lift. I was able to spend some time in the bright hallways, since light no longer bothered my eyes so much.

Life in 4A

My tolerance for sitting upright also started to improve about six weeks after my surgery. Until then I requested to be helped into bed right after supper, and my visitors would converse with me while I was in bed. Once I had the stamina to be upright for longer, I started spending the evenings in the lounge playing games with my visitors. On every unit the hospital has a cozy little lounge that is furnished with couches and a round table with four chairs. It was nicely decorated and made me feel as though I were no longer in a hospital. I would play games there every evening.

Boruch Hashem I wasn't affected cognitively by my surgery, so I enjoyed games that challenged my mind. I also tried to play games with small pieces, since they provided good practice for improving my fine motor coordination. I played Rummikub, Othello, Blokus, Scrabble, and card games. Playing games helped me keep sane, and I looked forward to these sessions each day.

Meals and Visitors

Until about a month into my rehabilitation, I could not feed myself. I don't remember how I managed my meals in the beginning, before a rotation of visitors was set up for me. I have only one clear memory of a nurse's aide feeding me one evening. I was in bed and my supper was a prepackaged kosher meal, which consisted of Salisbury steak, mashed potatoes and overcooked green beans. I remember the aide shoveling the food into my mouth so fast that I barely had time to swallow. When she finished, I said to her, "Please feed the next patient slower."

"Why didn't you tell me to slow down?" she asked.

"I couldn't," I replied. "Every time I opened my mouth, you stuffed food into it!"

For the first five weeks that I was in Scenic View, I ate the prepackaged kosher meals for lunch and supper. The food wasn't bad; it was just extremely boring to eat the same food twice a day, day in and day out, without much variation. A friend who visited quite often took it upon herself to arrange home cooked suppers for me. Every evening someone brought supper and stayed to keep me company and help me eat. Since Bikur Cholim volunteers brought a sandwich every day for lunch, I was soon eating the hospital food only for breakfast.

I had a hard time drinking from a cup, and whenever I used a straw, I aspirated some of the liquid. The hospital gave eight-ounce bottles of water with the food tray. I asked my husband to bring some water bottles with sports tops, from which I could drink easily. I transferred the sports tops to the small water bottles, which were much easier for me to handle, and drank all my drinks out of them.

When people first started sending me suppers, they sent enough for three people. I didn't know what to do with the leftovers, so I sent it home with my visitor. If it was something I knew my husband liked, I saved it for him, since he usually visited every night. It took a couple of weeks to finally get normal size portions, and the leftovers didn't go to waste anymore.

After supper, one or two visitors came, depending on their schedule. During the first six weeks, when I was usually in

Life in 4A

bed at that time, I always asked people to sit near the foot of my bed. It was hard for me to look sideways. When I was sitting in the wheelchair, I asked people to sit directly in front of me. If they were standing, I would have to crane my neck to see them and that was a big strain.

Most of my visitors were people I had never met before. I was relatively new to Monsey, and I did not have much of a social network yet. I met many new people, and made a number of friends. I was quite impressed by the scores of individuals who took the time and effort to visit a complete stranger. I don't remember them all, but I will be forever grateful for the great *chessed* they did for me.

Each morning, the first visitor of the day arrived between seven and eight. Visiting hours began at eleven, but the nurses bent the rules for me. My visitor would wash me *negel vasser* and say *birchos hashachar* out loud, while I answered, "Amen." I was still in bed at that time in the morning, since I had to wait for the nurse to re-bandage my burn. Consequently, I had to be fed breakfast, since I could only feed myself when I was sitting upright at a table. After breakfast, my visitor would stay with me until my first therapy session at eight thirty.

Shortly after therapy, between eleven thirty and twelve, the next person usually showed up. When I came back to my room, before the visitor arrived, I just sat there and waited, feeling horrible, lonely and bored. Many times I called a nurse to take me to the bathroom simply because I hated being alone even for a few minutes in my state. Usually a Bikur Cholim volunteer would come around then and bring me a sandwich.

My visitor stayed until around two o'clock, when I would go to bed and rest until my afternoon therapy. My schedule changed a little from time to time, but generally, I had visitors four times each day: during breakfast, lunch, supper, and then in the evening until nine p.m., when visiting hours ended.

At some point, I started watching television. I didn't actually enjoy it, and I couldn't find anything decent to watch; however, it was the only way to keep myself occupied. The TV was suspended from the ceiling over the bed on a large hinged bracket. Before I left for therapy, I asked one of the nurses to put it into place for me, so I could reach it from the wheelchair when I returned. When I finished my therapy for the day at three thirty, I usually watched TV until my visitor arrived with supper.

I fed myself supper with the help of my company. Depending on the food, they either cut it up for me or helped me get it onto my spoon or fork. There were many foods I couldn't manage and didn't bother eating. I had a hard time with cut up vegetable salad, rice, meatballs and spaghetti, and any soft food that would fall off my fork. The easiest food for me to eat was schnitzel. I mentioned this to my friend who arranged the suppers, and before I knew it, I had schnitzel every night! I then told her I could have anything for supper, because I didn't want the same thing every night.

When visitors arrived, they had to stop at the security desk, where they received a sticker with the unit number they were visiting. Visitors had to wear the sticker on their shirt. I was in unit 4A, and between my husband and the women from Bikur Cholim, I had at least six visitors each day. The security guards kept a pile of stickers with 4A written on it. Whenever a *frum*-looking person approached the desk, they automatically assumed the visitor was for me and pulled out a sticker for 4A.

Since most of my visitors were people whom I had never met, it took some time until we became acquainted and I learned their names. My mother suggested that I have a guest book for everyone to write in and sign. My sister in-law bought one for me, and I started asking everyone to write in it. I was not able to read it then, but I told everyone that I would read it when I was better.

Personal Care

The staff showered patients and washed their hair twice a week. On other days, we were given a bed bath. A nurse's aide washed us down with disposable washcloths and a basin of soapy water. I always felt soapy after these "baths." I don't think one can be properly rinsed with a wet washcloth.

When I was showered, the aide used a special wheelchair that rolled directly into the shower. I felt cleaner after a shower than after a bed bath, but I still never felt as clean as when I was finally able to wash myself on my own.

After my surgery, I didn't brush my teeth for some time. I was simply too weak. After a few weeks, I was able to do it again. I tried to floss every day, too. I used Plackers, which are small plastic disposable flossers. They are used with only one hand, so they were ideal for me. I also used an electric toothbrush, so brushing my teeth was not too difficult either. I only needed someone to prepare a cup of water and put the toothpaste on my toothbrush. The hospital rooms had sinks without cabinets underneath, so I was able to roll my wheelchair under the sink and get close enough as I brushed. Although it was tedious and awkward, I managed to brush and floss every day.

For the first six weeks, I went into bed at around six o'clock in the evening. I was exhausted by then. I would brush my teeth right after supper. At around eleven o'clock each night I felt hungry again, but since I had brushed my teeth already, I did not want to eat. Besides, I had no way of getting myself any food.

I was used to washing my face properly before going to bed each night, but I could not do it on my own. My husband brought pre-soaped face washcloths. They must be wet before using, but they were folded into four and I could not spread them out. I tried to unfold them, but found that I just could not manage. On some nights, I would ask one of my visitors to wash my face for me, but I did not always feel comfortable making the request. I usually went to sleep without having my face washed, and it gave me an unclean feeling. I broke out in pimples around my nose and on my chin. It was horrible that I could not take care of some of my basic needs.

Patients wore their own clothes during the day and the hospital gown at night. I had arrived in the winter, so I had a bunch of turtlenecks and a few basic black skirts. I wore these every day, including Shabbos. Food always fell onto me during meals, and my clothes had to be washed constantly. Though the hospital had a laundry room, I was unable to do my laundry on my own. Twice a week I sent my dirty

Life in 4A

laundry with one of my visitors to Zehava Pearl to be washed. She sent everything back fresh and neatly folded. When the weather became warmer, I wore button down shirts, which Zehava always ironed for me.

When I first came to the hospital, I wore regular loafers, but I needed more support, and my therapists recommended lace up shoes. The only lace up shoes I had at home were the white sneakers I had worn to my wedding. My husband brought them for me, and I told everyone I was wearing my wedding shoes. I even had a wedding picture of me wearing them in my room.

I could not wash my hands often and rarely felt clean. I was unable to lift my left hand up by itself, and it was too heavy for my right hand to hold it and dry it at the same time. I couldn't dry my right hand properly either. I had to use my left one to do that. I would roll my right hand back and forth over a rough commercial paper towel, but that only superficially dried it. I could not dry between my fingers well either. Nurses would not assist me, since their philosophy was to let patients do as much as they could on their own. Even if the quality of care was not as good, they believed it was preferable for patients to do these tasks themselves. They called this independence and it frustrated me enormously.

While in the hospital, I was taught to put on the sleeve of my weak side first when dressing myself. The weak arm is not as flexible, so once the sleeve is on that side, the other arm, which can move more easily, can still get into the other sleeve. While undressing, the order is reversed, and the stronger side is removed first.

My fingernails grew and I was unable to cut them myself. A friend arranged for a manicurist to come and cut them for me. I then asked her to continue coming about every two weeks.

Nurse's Aides

The hospital had about five nurse's aides per shift. These aides were there to help patients bathe and dress in the morning, to assist them while using the bathroom, to get them ready for bed at night, and to help them in and out of bed.

The patients were divided between the aides, and each one was primarily responsible for "her" patients' care. This system allowed us to have the same aides again and again, and I developed a few nice relationships over time.

I had one steady morning aide who truly made my stay in the hospital much more tolerable. Her name was Angel, and she had a happy, outgoing personality. She was always laughing, and I would hear her voice ringing through the halls in the hospital. Angel worked five days a week, and on the days that she wasn't there, things were just not the same. The other aides performed their tasks just as well, but with Angel I had a special relationship.

Angel knew how I liked things done, and while she helped me wash and dress, I would chat with her and discuss all the ridiculous thoughts I had been pondering through my wakeful hours the previous night.

Angel would affectionately call me "kiddo." She was almost old enough to be my mother, and we had a parent-

Life in 4A

child relationship in the type of care she gave me. I never minded when she called me that. In contrast, when the therapist who was a few years younger called me by a pet name, it felt phony and was unappreciated.

Even with the help of nurse's aides, there was still much that frustrated me. I couldn't fix my clothes if something wasn't put on right. Often my skirt was twisted with the side seams in the wrong place. It was nerve-racking when my socks slid down and I could not pull them up. My snood regularly slid back, and I was not able to fix it. The worst was when I went to the bathroom, and the nurse's aide didn't adjust my clothes properly afterwards. I was left feeling uncomfortable for hours. In fact, out of frustration, I wrote the following poem on April 23, 2006:

> *This whole situation is hard to bear,*
> *Sitting all day in a wheelchair,*
> *I can't even pull up my own underwear.*
> *I've already shed many a tear.*
> *I can't wait until this time next year,*
> *When I will be all better,*
> *Good as new.*
> *How long I'll be here,*
> *I haven't a clue.*
> *But looking back,*
> *I'll say the time flew.*

STRUGGLE TO THE SUMMIT

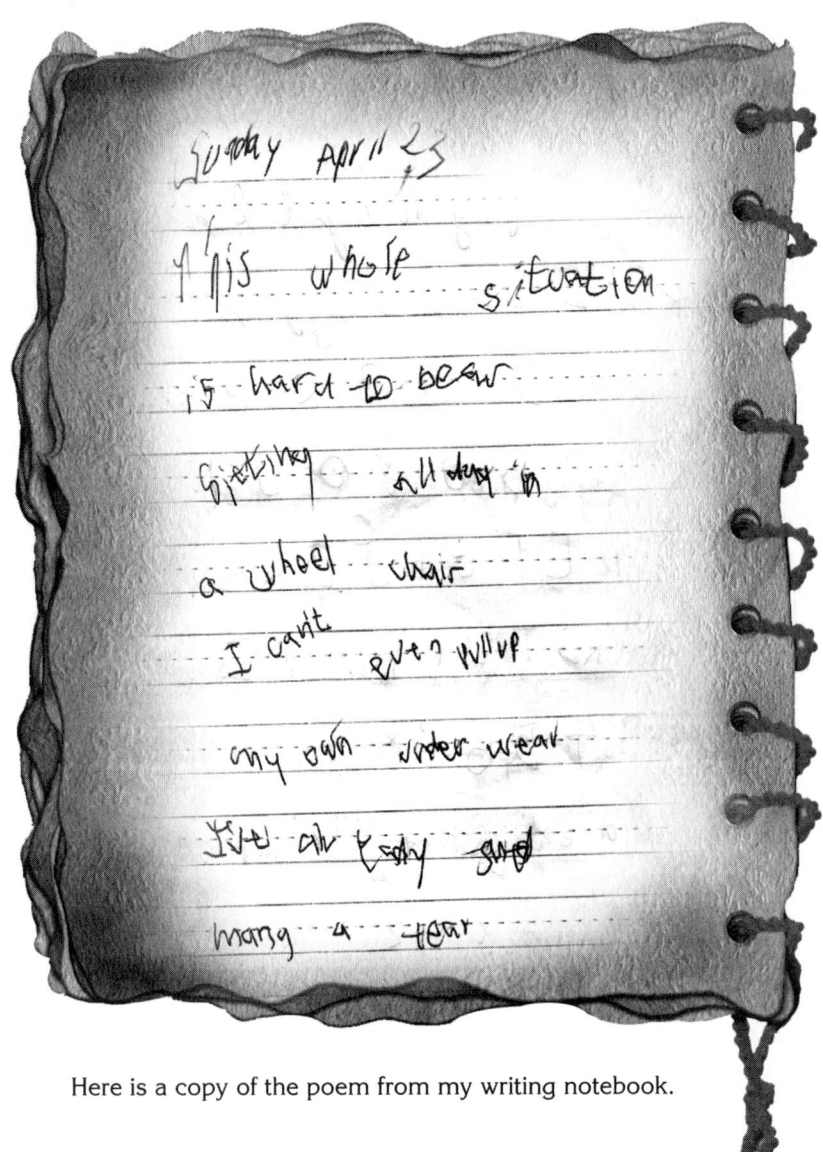

Here is a copy of the poem from my writing notebook.

Life in 4A

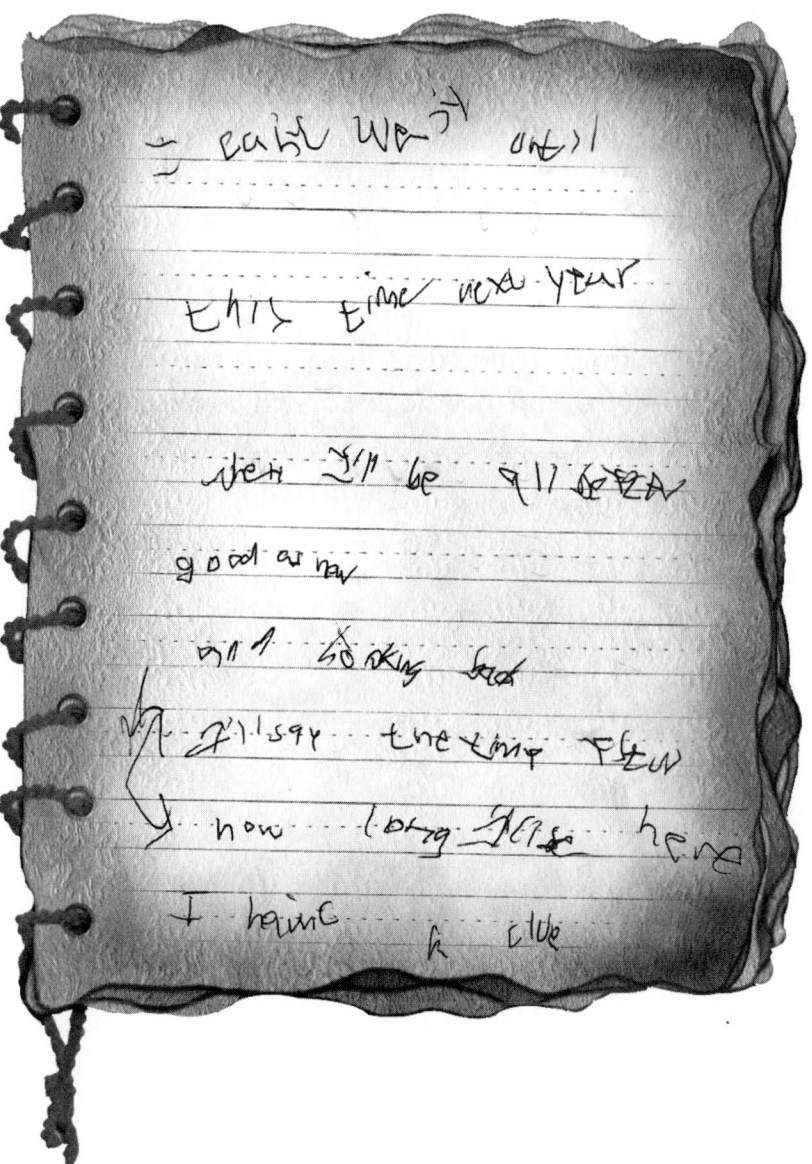

My whole situation was mortifying. I am usually put together and on top of things, and now I was stuck in a situation where my physical appearance was totally beyond my control. Whenever I would see myself in the mirror, I would start crying. I looked awful. Besides my sometimes unkempt appearance, my face was puffed up from the steroids, and I had broken out in acne. I also kept one eye closed all the time, which caused my face to be lopsided. I tried not to look in the mirror. It depressed me terribly.

During those moments, the mountain seemed to grow ever larger. It was hard to remain focused, and continue believing that I would ever to make it all the way to the top.

Life in 4A

My mother remembers:

My dear daughter, Rivkah,

You were always a doer. As the oldest girl in the family, you were my right hand "man." You capably and reliably took care of your younger siblings. When you were only twelve, I was sick Erev Sukkos, and you cooked for the entire yom tov.

In tenth grade you tackled a project using a jigsaw. You cut a three dimensional tree out of wood, for your school's Derech Eretz expo. It was so impressive. You were head of sewing for the school play. You sewed most of your Shabbos outfits, and even some for your sisters and me. You helped cook, bake and set up for various family simchos. You were a great help to me all around.

When you were married at a relatively later age, you seemed truly blessed. You had two children in quick succession; your husband was well employed, and you even owned your own home. I felt very happy for you.

Then, at our Chanukah get-together, you told us that you had been having some numbness around your mouth, and that it wasn't the first time you had experienced this. You didn't seem too concerned at the time and told us you planned to visit your doctor about it. We went home, and afterwards you were unreachable for about two weeks. When you finally called, you said that you had been in the hospital, but hadn't told us so as not to alarm us. You explained that your symptoms had gotten considerably worse, and they now caused double vision and clumsiness. You had seen a neurologist and had learned that your symptoms were caused by a Cavernous Angioma in your brainstem that had bled, causing stroke-like symptoms. You had to have surgery as soon as possible, since another episode of bleeding could render you much worse, or even be fatal, chas V'shalom.

The surgery was scheduled for early February. Tatty was afraid we might not see you in your normal state for a long time (or chas v'shalom, ever again), so we visited you a week before your surgery. When we arrived at your home, we saw that your condition had seriously deteriorated. You had a clumsy gait and kept dropping and spilling things.

After your surgery, I called you in Arizona as soon as you were able to talk on the phone. I was terrified as to what your condition would be. Your speech was slurred and unclear, and you spoke in a monotone without any expression whatsoever. I was relieved to hear, however, that you were cognitively intact, and your memory was unaffected.

Ten days later, your husband Yisroel brought you back and admitted you to a rehab hospital not far from your home. We were unable to make the trip to see you right away. I first visited you about a month after your surgery, and although I knew what to expect, I was greatly disheartened when I saw you. My beautiful daughter's face was all puffed up and distorted from the steroids. You were propped up in a wheelchair that you couldn't move on your own. You were always uncomfortable. Light bothered you, so you kept your eyes closed. You needed help for all your personal needs and were robbed of your dignity. Your moods could change from moment to moment. Sometimes you would suddenly start crying, and your emotions were out of control.

It was upsetting for me to see you like that. You were always a very strong and determined person. I felt helpless and inadequate when I saw you struggling. I did not know how to help you.

In order to take a few steps during therapy, you needed two attendants to help, one holding you on each side. You also had one aide who followed with a wheelchair, in case you would need to sit down suddenly. You were sweating profusely from the effort of doing something most people take for granted, from when they are only toddlers.

Twice I stayed with you in the rehab center for Shabbos, together with my sister. We tried to cheer you up by singing zemiros, reading to you and bringing home-cooked foods. When you were somewhat better, I played Boggle with you. You asked me to use my left hand, since writing for you was still slow and difficult. You didn't want me to have the unfair advantage of being able to write faster.

Every time I saw you, I saw your improvement and your determination to get better, as quickly as possible. I am very proud of your determination and willpower. I cannot wait to see you running your home independently. I am happy to see your old capabilities slowly coming back. Within your limitations, you are still the doer that you used to be. I believe that other people in a similar situation, who don't work as hard as you to get better, may never reach their complete potential. I hope you will be an inspiration to others, who would otherwise give up hope.

With Hashem's help and your perseverance, you have come a very long way. I daven and wish for you a complete recovery.

With lots of love,
Mommy

7
Rehabilitation

Therapists

The therapists at Scenic View Rehab Center have an excellent reputation, but in the state I was in, I was not always satisfied with their performance. Being a patient was awfully degrading, especially since I could do so little. I felt like a young child who had therapists "in charge" of me, telling me what to do. Just like any two people in a relationship, therapists are not always compatible with all their patients.

There was one therapist in particular, whose approach grated on my nerves. She would call me "Lovey" repeatedly during our sessions, and I felt that her pet name and feigned affection were demeaning. I'm a straight-forward, frank person and, I did not appreciate the insincerity. I never said anything about it. I wasn't clearheaded enough at the time to pinpoint exactly what bothered me so much. Besides, it took so much effort to formulate my thoughts into words, that I would have just started crying.

I'm sharing my frustration to spread awareness of this issue to therapists and caretakers who work with adults. It is important to remember that when someone's physical body is not functioning properly, one cannot assume that his or her intelligence has been affected. Adult patients are not children, and it is especially humiliating for them to be treated in such a manner.

Another therapist, with whom I loved to work, was kind and sensitive, and she really treated me as an equal. If she spoke to me when I was sitting in the wheelchair, she would squat down and talk to me at eye level. This was very thoughtful and considerate of her. It was extremely hard for me, with my impaired eyesight, to have a conversation with people while craning my neck to look up at them.

Indeed, a therapist must be exceptionally sensitive and compassionate when dealing with people who suddenly find themselves in such a difficult situation. It is hard to describe just how helpless I felt. I often became frustrated during my therapy sessions, and I would start crying all the time. I was used to being extremely capable and able to do almost anything I set out to achieve. My occupational therapist would lose her patience with me and try to rationalize and explain that I have to try harder. She said I was making nice progress, but I disagreed.

A few incidences stand out in my memory. Once, for example, when I started to have some movement in my left hand and was able to grasp some things, my OT put a basket

Rehabilitation

of clothes on the table in front of me and told me to fold them. I had no idea where or how to start using only my right hand. I kept on trying with one hand. It didn't even occur to me to use my left hand. In my mind it was useless, and I treated it as if it wasn't there. I started crying out of sheer frustration. I thought the whole thing was absurd.

"I don't see the point of this exercise," I told her. "I will anyways not be folding any laundry until I am able to do it properly."

"If you don't try you will never learn how to do it," she replied.

I disagreed with her. I felt that as soon as my hands would start to move properly, I would be able to fold laundry.

Another time, my therapist brought me to Scenic View's small lifelike apartment, which has a kitchen and bedroom. It is used to help patients prepare for when they will go home. Once we were there, my therapist ordered me to fry an egg. "Everything is labeled," she said. "Find what you need, bring it to the counter and fry an egg."

The therapist stood and watched while I struggled to find a frying pan, spatula, oil, a bowl and fork, and an egg from the refrigerator. The sink and stovetop were set into the counter and there weren't any cabinets underneath, so I could easily sit in a wheelchair, put everything on the counter and get close enough to work. I had to crack the egg in a bowl and scramble it with a fork. It was hard for me to crack the egg properly with one clumsy hand, and eggshells fell into the bowl. I poured too much oil in the pan, but I wasn't going to eat the egg anyway. My coordination was so impaired that I was afraid I would burn myself. I managed to fry the egg, and afterwards my therapist told me to wash all the dishes, which was another almost impossible task.

Sometime during this task, I became frustrated and started sobbing. I thought it was one of the cruelest and most degrading therapy sessions.

During another therapy session that annoyed me, my therapist gave me a newspaper and a paper with questions. The questions were about different sports events and TV shows. Aside from the fact that I was not familiar with them, I had no idea where to start looking for the answers. It was cumbersome to handle the large newspaper with just my right hand. My hand also became black from the ink, and it was difficult for me to wash it afterwards.

So long as my therapist had me do things that worked on my movement and fine motor coordination with toys and games, I was happy to cooperate. As soon as she had me do ordinary housekeeping activities, I fell apart. I had always prided myself in how well I ran my household and how efficient and capable I was. When I was reminded of all I was unable to do, I just broke down crying.

One time my husband brought a large tray of brownies for me to give to my therapist. The tray was awkward and too heavy for me to bring to the therapy room. I told my therapist about it and asked her to come to my room and get it. Instead she had me move my wheelchair with my feet all the way to my room and carry the tray of brownies on my lap back to the therapy room. Then she gave me four plates and a spatula and told me to divide them. Afterwards, I had to carry one plate at a time on my lap to the nurses' station, the speech therapy room, the physical therapy office and the occupational therapy office.

I was so angry with the therapist for making me do this. Though I hid my emotions, I was absolutely seething inside! I didn't like getting my hands dirty, and I had brownie mush under all my fingernails that I was unable to clean.

Whenever I worked with small pieces, it was inevitable that some would fall onto the floor. Sometimes, when my OT would be in a benevolent mood, she picked them up. Usually she ordered me to wheel over to where the piece fell, lock the brakes of my wheelchair, and bend down to pick it up.

I was wearing a seat belt, so toppling out of the wheelchair was not a worry, but I hated when she made me do this. It felt extremely demeaning. Nonetheless, my therapist insisted that small pieces are a choking hazard, and since I had small children at home, I would have to be careful.

I thought that this was a ridiculous reason. There was no way I would be left alone with my young children. By making me pick up the small pieces that fell, did she think she would teach me to become more coordinated? I felt her approach was wrong and insensitive.

Physical Therapy

Every time I tried walking, my left ankle twisted, my foot turned in, and my left knee locked backwards in an awkward position. My therapist had me fitted for an AFO (ankle foot orthotic), which is a special brace that went from my toes up to my knee. My ankle was held in a fixed position, so I would no longer twist it. This brace also prevented my knee from locking backwards.

To make the AFO, my physical therapist took me down to the ground level of the hospital, where they had a department which made prosthetic limbs and special braces and orthotics. The orthotist took a mold of my foot and leg up to my knee, and from that he fashioned a custom brace.

I had to wear the AFO for one hour the first day and for an additional hour each day thereafter so that my skin would not react badly to it. I did not like to wear it. The hospital was already stifling hot, and the brace caused me to sweat even more. I also had a hard time propelling my wheelchair. With my ankle fixed by the brace, I couldn't bend it and walk my foot. I ended up using it only during therapy sessions.

My progress was slow with physical therapy. My balance was more or less nonexistent. I needed three people to walk with me each time I practiced; one supported me on each side, helping me stay upright, and the third followed with the wheelchair, so I could sit down as soon as I could no longer continue.

Due to my left leg's weakness, I was gripped by a subconscious fear, and I had a hard time putting weight in it. This caused me to feel like my right foot was stuck to the floor. In order to pick up one leg you have to shift all your weight to the other leg, and I couldn't figure out how to do this. It was astounding! I had been walking for almost thirty years, yet it was so hard to learn again.

Rehabilitation

To complicate matters, I also had severe ataxia, meaning that my leg seemed to have a mind of its own. It wouldn't necessary land where I intended to place it. I had ataxia in my upper body as well. If I was leaning a little too forward and I tried to correct myself, I usually ended up throwing my torso too far back.

I used a hemi-walker at the time, and it was difficult for me to figure out where to place it for each step. My therapist showed me again and again. It was so hard for me to grasp. She started to think I had a memory problem. I usually ended up crying out of frustration during therapy. Here I was an intelligent adult, and I could not grasp the basics of walking.

About six weeks into therapy, I developed a new problem that is difficult to describe. The surgery was in my brainstem, which dictates the whole body's equilibrium. During the healing process, a complete sense of disorientation would periodically come over me. It can best be described with the word vertigo, but it doesn't do justice to the feeling. It wasn't dizziness or spinning. I felt as if my surroundings became distorted. The floor and walls didn't look right. They seemed to be moving in waves.

This sensation would appear usually when I was trying to walk during therapy, and sometimes even when I was sitting and moving my wheelchair. Logically, I knew that the distortion was all my perception, and I was on a solid, flat surface. However, when it happened while I was trying to walk, I could not continue. This lasted for about two and a half weeks, and then it finally cleared up. Once I was over that setback, I started progressing at a slightly faster rate.

Occupational Therapy

I had three half-hour sessions of occupational therapy each day. In the beginning, they were not too tiring, because my OT worked on my right hand. Even though this was my better hand, she focused on it exclusively at first in order to increase my independence and enable me to have at least one somewhat functional hand. I had no trouble moving that hand, but I could barely perform even simple tasks.

While my right hand improved, I still could not move my left hand at all. Once the therapists began focusing on it, my therapy sessions became much more challenging. Some mobility returned to my hand, but my progress was slow and the slightest movement required much energy. In the beginning, when I moved my fingers I would feel the muscles in my upper arm moving. It was a strange feeling. I never realized how many muscles were involved in one small movement.

As I was able to move my left hand more, the therapy sessions became harder and more strenuous. Just picking up large pegs with my left hand and putting them into a peg board caused me to tremble and sweat from exertion. I thought it would become easier with time, but as I was able to do more, my therapist gave me harder tasks to accomplish.

As I regained movement in my left side, I startled at the slightest noise: a telephone ring, a cough or even when the button on my tape recorder popped up. My left side would jump uncontrollably. Likewise, whenever I sneezed, my left arm and hand would jump as well. It was strange not to be in control of my own body's movements.

Rehabilitation

Although at some point I was able to stretch all my fingers somewhat normally, I could only stretch my left thumb at a 45 degree angle, instead of the normal 90 degrees. My therapist advised me to stretch my thumb out with my right hand, warning me that otherwise the thumb might never regain its former range. From then on, I constantly moved it in and out, often with the help of my right hand. With time, I was able to flex it more and more. Eventually I was able to stretch it by itself to the full 90 degrees.

I was able to make a fist and grasp a ball, but I was unable to throw it. I could not release the ball, although I concentrated on moving my arms to throw it. I would try again and again. I actually found this funny and would laugh when trying to throw a ball.

When I was in bed, I had a whole series of different movements I did with my left arm and hand. I used the TV that was hanging on a hinge from the ceiling above my bed for exercise. I would hook my fingers around the handle and swing the TV back and forth with my left hand. I had to lift my left arm and bend my fingers around the handle with my right hand. I couldn't do it with my left hand alone.

All the nurses and therapists called my right side my good side. To me, it was my bad side, and my left was my worse side. Since I was able to move it, everyone assumed that it worked fine. Truthfully, however, my right hand was very weak. It lacked dexterity and was quite useless. I could not even pull up my blanket, which was a mere lightweight sheet. Even waving or pointing a finger was awkward. Lifting my hand up to my face to scratch an itch was too cumbersome for me when I was sitting. It was hard to lift the weight of my own hand. When I was sitting in the wheelchair, simply holding the telephone up to my ear was tiresome and draining.

One time a visitor brought me a cinnamon bun. I wanted to break off small pieces to eat it, but that requires two hands, and I was unable to do it. I decided to pick up the bun with my right hand instead and bite into it, but I was so weak I could not lift it to my mouth. I remember laughing at the incident, but in truth, it actually upset me.

In life, there are two ways to react to a situation; you can either laugh or cry. Sometimes, I just laughed.

In order to strengthen my arms, my OT taught me to do exercises that involved linking my hands. While they were in this position, I had to lift my left arm up over my head with my right hand. She taught me to do this while sitting in the wheelchair. I was extremely weak and had poor upper body control, so I toppled over sideways when doing this exercise. I also had an especially hard time linking my two hands together, since I had absolutely no movement yet in my left hand.

First, I needed to place my left hand onto my lap using my right hand. Even then, because the dexterity of my right hand was so poor, it would take a few minutes' attempt to finally succeed. I tried this exercise while reclining in bed, and it was much easier. Once my hands were linked together, I moved my left arm with my right arm in a variety of movements: up and down, side to side and diagonally.

I was constantly on the lookout for more ideas, to help improve the mobility of my left hand. One afternoon I just had no energy to get out of bed, so I did not call for a nurse's aide to help me get up. It was my responsibility to get myself to therapy. When I failed to show up, my therapist came to my room. She had an exasperated look on her face. Before she could voice her annoyance, I asked her to show me exercises to do in bed on my own. She showed me a whole series of exercises to work on my left arm and hand. I started to do these exercises a few times each day when I was in bed. I also opened and closed my left fist and spread my fingers apart and back together again. I moved whatever I could as often as possible.

Other Therapies

The therapists in Scenic View were constantly on my case. They kept telling me to open my eyes, but the double vision was unbearable. I preferred to keep one eye closed; it was the only way I could tolerate seeing. It looked like both of my eyes were closed, because my second eye was only barely open. My occupational therapist wanted me to wear a patch and gave me one on an elastic band, but it never stayed in place. Since I was crying so often and the patch was constantly wet, I jokingly referred to it as my tear catcher.

The steroids also caused my vision to blur, so this aggravated my vision problems. When I first opened an eye, I saw clearly for ten or fifteen seconds, and then everything would turn blurry. When that happened, I switched and opened my other eye. I was constantly switching back and forth from eye to eye, and it was an enormous strain. Many times, I just kept my eyes closed. When I had company, I often apologized that it was too hard to keep my eyes open, and we conversed while I kept them closed. I also found it hard to make eye contact. The most comfortable position for me was to look down at the floor.

Post surgery my speech was unclear and slurred. I could only speak in a monotone, and my voice was deeper than before. I assume the change in my voice, was due to the fact that my left vocal cord wasn't moving. As a result, communicating was taxing for me. Nevertheless, I was always a big talker, so that didn't stop me.

I had two sessions of speech therapy each day. One session was one-on-one with a therapist, while the other was in a group setting. The latter was called oral motor group; we were a group of four patients and one therapist, and we did all kinds of mouth and tongue exercises together.

One of the exercises entailed saying "oh eeeee, oh eeeee" very slowly and drawn out. I felt like I had joined a cult and was chanting a mantra. This group was in the early morning, and I was usually not out of bed yet. After just a few days, I stopped going. I figured my speech would improve by itself with time.

My speech therapist worked with me on my eating and articulation. For some odd reason, I took large bites and swallowed quickly, without chewing my food well. She advised me to slow down. She also instructed me to speak more slowly and pronounce each syllable. I was used to speaking quickly and clearly, and it was extremely frustrating as I tried to slow down.

In the afternoon, when I was resting in bed, I had my speech therapy session in my room. My therapist asked me

Rehabilitation

to read different passages aloud, and she told me to pause after every few words to take a breath. It was hard to hold the paper up while lying in bed. My right hand was weak, and even though a paper is lightweight, it kept folding and falling. Due to my double vision, it was difficult to read altogether. I kept one eye closed the whole time and constantly lost the place.

These sessions were exhausting. The therapist would also record me and then play it back for me to hear. I sounded awful and found it discouraging to listen to myself on tape.

After about two weeks, I decided to stop my speech therapy altogether. It was enervating, and I felt that I didn't gain enough to justify how much it wore me out. I didn't have much stamina to begin with. I wanted to preserve my energy for occupational and physical therapy, which were both also exhausting.

I did not attempt to write immediately after my surgery; I tried only a few weeks later, after my steroid dosage was lowered too soon. As a result, my right hand had suddenly lost coordination. I had tremors and could barely hold a pen. The first time I tried writing, I had almost no control, and my writing was completely illegible. The tremors caused my writing to be shaky.

My therapist suggested I get a notebook and write in it every day. I followed her advice and saw my handwriting improve with time. The following is one of the first pages from my writing notebook. It is legible but very shaky.

About six weeks into my rehab, I joined two other group therapies. One was called fine motor group, which was a

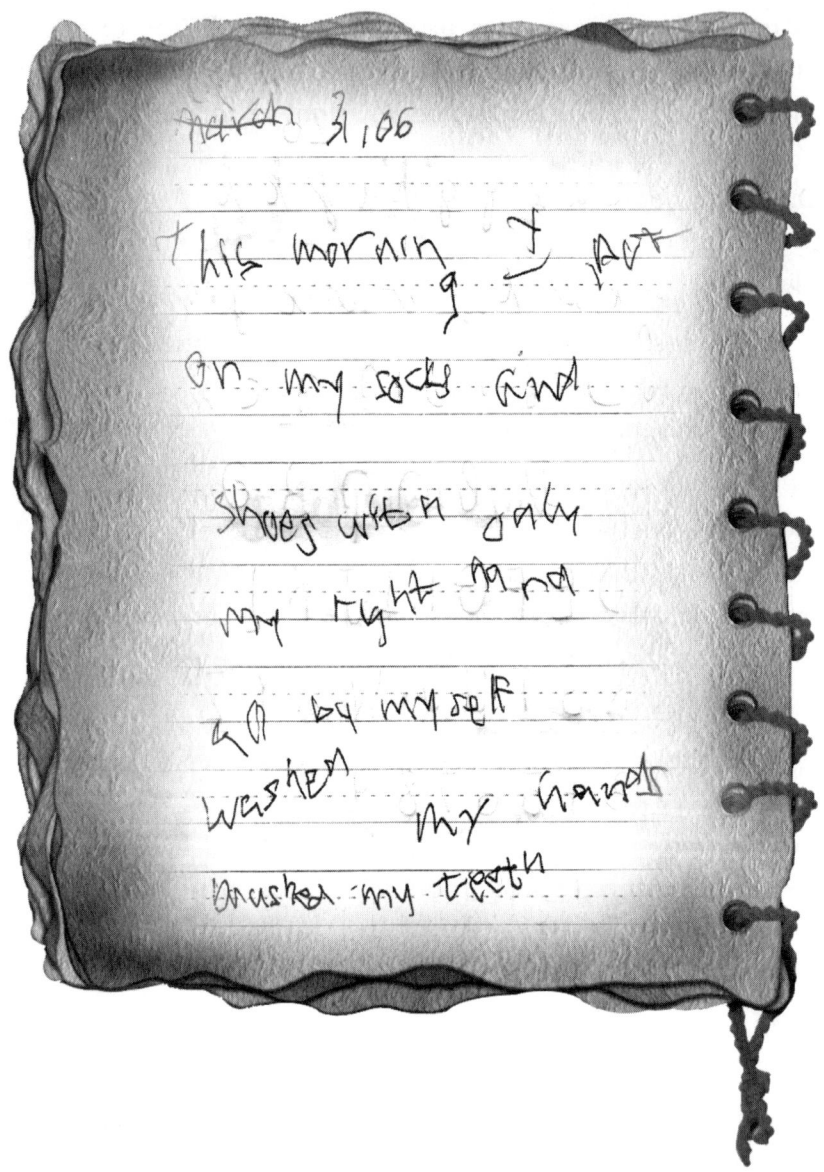

half hour session with about six patients led by two OT's. We played games with small pieces or cards primarily using the weaker hand. I enjoyed these sessions; they were not too intense and provided me with a social outlet.

The other therapy I was given was called transfer class. It included a physical therapist, a PT assistant and three patients. In this class, we were taught the most efficient technique of transferring out of the wheelchair and into another chair. We first met in the dining room, and then we were taken downstairs to the hospital chapel, where there was a variety of chairs to practice getting in and out of. During the entire half hour, each patient transferred into a chair, and back into the wheelchair only two or three times. It was exhausting, and we had to rest in between each transfer.

At one point I was the only patient left in the group. By then, the weather outside had turned mild. The hospital had well-kept grounds with beautiful landscaping and a gazebo with comfortable wooden armchairs. The therapists would take me outside for this session, and I transferred back and forth into these wooden chairs. When I rested between each transfer, we sat and chatted. I enjoyed these sessions immensely. I was able to escape the stifling hospital atmosphere and breathe the fresh air outside. I had twenty minutes each day to cool off, and I felt truly revived.

F.I.M. Scores

I wasn't fond of most aspects of rehab, but what I resented most was F.I.M. scores. F.I.M. stands for **F**unction **I**ndependence **M**easure. These scores were primarily for the medical insurance company to gauge a patient's progress.

According to these scores, it was determined whether to continue paying for the patient's hospital stay.

For OT, the score depended on two things: grooming and eating independently. Grooming included showering, brushing one's teeth and hair, and shaving for men. My OT would instruct me to take a shower, and she would see how much I could do on my own.

She wheeled me into the shower, and set up shampoo, body wash and washcloths. She then turned on the water and expected me to wash by myself. I had one functionally inadequate hand to work with, and a low-pressured hand held showerhead. I was supposed to wet my hair, lather it up and rinse it all myself. These were all impossible tasks for me, since, to accomplish them, one must be able to move around the hair while spraying water. Otherwise, only the top layer gets wet, especially, if the water pressure is low.

This upset me greatly. I wanted to be showered properly, but could simply not do it on my own. The therapist acted as though I was unreasonable for being upset. If I told her I wasn't rinsed well, she would tell me, "Rinse more."

As embarrassing as it was, I felt that as long as I needed someone to come into the shower and give me all my supplies why couldn't that person assist me with washing too?! I was not yet showering independently anyway. To me it seemed unreasonable and a waste of time to do it myself. The philosophy of therapy, however, is to let the patients do as much as they can on their own. This boosts the F.I.M. score, and makes the therapist feel that she is doing her job.

Rehabilitation

My OT also taught me how to put on my socks and shoes using only my right hand. First, she put elastic laces in my sneakers, so I would be able to put them on without having to tie the laces. Then she propped me up to a sitting position in bed, so I was able to reach my feet. I learned how to first put all five fingers of my good hand into the opening of my sock and then place the hand over my toes. I then slowly inched the sock up over my foot and up my leg, going back and forth from side to side, as I pulled it up. Similarly, I learned to put on shoes with one hand.

I was opposed to learning how to get dressed this way. I was sure my condition was only temporary, and I still needed help with basic dressing. I did not see the point of learning how to put on my socks and shoes by myself when someone still had to position me properly, prepare them and hand them to me. It was so much quicker and more efficient if one of the nurse's aides did it. In addition, I wanted to work on improving my left hand's function, not on learning to do things one-handedly.

My OT, however, insisted that this brought me one step closer to being independent. I disagreed with her. In my opinion, for someone who had become permanently disabled, it is important to learn to compensate. I, on the other hand, would eventually be able to do it on my own and would have assistance until then. It seemed pointless to struggle.

After a few weeks, I was able to feed myself, but not without making a mess. I was barely able to grasp finger foods, so eating foods such as grapes or baby carrots, was difficult for me. When I was sitting upright at a table, I was able to navigate the food to my mouth. I could not always get the food on the spoon or fork, and once I did, there was no guarantee it would stay there until it reached my mouth. By the end of the day, there was always plenty of food on my clothes. I felt like a baby.

Even though there was marked improvement in how I moved my left side, my F.I.M. scores for OT didn't show any improvement. I still needed more or less the same amount of assistance with washing and dressing as when I first came to Scenic View.

For PT, F.I.M. scores are based on how much assistance one needs while walking. It depends on how many people were needed for support, and the distance one can walk before growing too tired. Here, my F.I.M. scores did not improve either. The quality of my walking did not change much for a while. It took a long time until I was able to increase my distance before I became too exhausted to continue. The most I was able to endure was about 150 feet.

Of course, it is hardly surprising that I so detested the F.I.M. scores. They never accurately reflected my progress and always left me feeling hopeless and dejected. They were towering obstacles on my climb, often obscuring my view of the mountaintop. Somehow, with perseverance and persistence, I managed to continue marching on.

Rehabilitation

My sister Hadassa remembers:

Dear Rivkah,

I still clearly remember that difficult, hectic week when you were first hospitalized. At the time, I was in nursing school and holding down a full-time job, when I suddenly found myself looking after your house and taking care of a toddler and infant, together with our brother Yaakov. I remember waking up every two hours to feed the baby at night; rushing to get everyone ready in the morning; driving your minivan to drop them off at your friend's house; running to work and school; hurrying home to serve supper and bathe the kids; falling into bed in exhaustion at night and then doing it all over again.

Your husband, Yisroel, rarely returned home to help with the children at bedtime; usually he was too busy caring for you and meeting with doctors. When you returned from Beth Israel, Yisroel hired Beatrice to care for the children. I moved back into my apartment after that and only returned to spend Shabbosos at your house.

After your surgery, I went to visit you at Scenic View. I remember how unsettling it was the first time I saw you. You were the one who had always held the family together and worried for all of us. Now, you were lying helplessly in bed, crying constantly. It was hard to see you like that and deal with the emotions it triggered. I wondered whether your mental and emotional state would ever be the same.

Thankfully, after those first difficult weeks, you began improving, and you focused resolutely on your recovery. You were popular with the nurses and visitors, and they were all moved by the motivational and inspirational quotes and pesukim you hung on the wall in your room. That alone reassured me that the old Rivkah was truly coming back.

Soon, my friend Blimi and I began spending Shabbos with you regularly. We tried not to focus on all the upsetting and challenging aspects of the situation and to make it a fun and enjoyable time. We played games, told jokes and tried to find the humor in the situation. Whether observing some of the more eccentric patients or noting some unusual activity at the hospital, we could always find something to smile about if we looked hard enough.

In truth, I usually prefer to spend Shabbos alone, curling up with a book, recharging my batteries. Nonetheless, I was happy to give up on my treasured personal time and be there for you. After all you have done for me and everyone else, I felt that it was the least I could do for you.

Rehabilitation

In the ensuing months, it was difficult to watch you struggle. The once competent, reliable Rivkah, was often helpless and discouraged. Before, no obstacle was too great for you, but now, you often complained that simple, everyday tasks were "just not possible" for you to do. Later, when you began announcing the smallest milestone with great enthusiasm, it was sometimes difficult for me to share in your happiness. How could I be happy when my indomitable sister, the rock we had always leaned on, was gleefully celebrating a sock pulled on independently, or five steps taken without support?

But Rivkah, you did celebrate each small step, and with time, we looked back and realized that, with these tiny strides, a large distance had been covered. You are still the strong, determined Rivkah, and I look forward to seeing where your courage and willpower will lead you.

With love,
Hadassah

8

Pesach Approaches

When I first came to Scenic View from Arizona, I had not seen my children for eleven days. I desperately wanted to see them, but it was difficult for my husband to arrange a good time for them to visit. He finally brought them, accompanied by Beatrice, about a week later. Libby acted shy and did not want to come near me. My baby did not seem to remember me, and he was happily bouncing on Beatrice's lap. I cried through the whole visit. I felt strange, as though they were not even my children, and was relieved when they left.

It was hard on both Libby and me; I was unable to interact with her, yet I reminded her of the mother she remembered. After she went home, she acted out and was miserable for days. Shloimy was too young to understand, and he was not affected at all.

Due to the ill effect the visit had on Libby, my husband was advised not to bring her again. I missed my children terribly, but in truth, the visit had only made me feel more inadequate. I tried not to think of my children and cried every time they were mentioned. I understood that it had been difficult for Libby, but I still cried and begged my husband to bring them. Just talking about them would start me crying. I longed for them so badly.

Beatrice took care of my children at home all week, and suppers continued to be sent for my family. My single brother Yaakov was staying at my house at the time, and he said *shema* with them every night. My sister Hadassa did the grocery shopping, making sure that my household had everything it needed. My husband drove Beatrice home on Fridays and picked her up each Motzei Shabbos. During the first few weeks, when my husband spent Shabbos in the hospital with me, either my brother and sister in-law or married friends moved into my house for Shabbos with their family, so that my children would have a normal Shabbos.

Finding people to stay with my children each Shabbos was becoming a hassle and besides, we wanted the children to be in a *yiddishe* atmosphere all week. We were very close with the Ehrmann family, and to our good fortune, they invited Beatrice and the children to move into their one bedroom basement apartment, which was vacant at the time. My husband immediately agreed to the plan and transported the children's cribs, clothes and other belongings to the apartment. Beatrice continued caring for my children there, but here they were also part of a wonderful *frum* household. My husband slept at home all week, and ate the Shabbos *seudos* at the Ehrmanns.

Pesach Approaches

Shortly before *Purim*, my mother in-law came from England to visit me. She also stayed at the Ehrmanns and was thus able to spend time with my children.

While my mother in-law was in town, she planned to visit a young woman named Zeldy Wasserman. Zeldy was originally from Russia, and during her teens, she had spent much time in my in-law's home while attending seminary in Gateshead. She had become like a member of the family and had formed a close bond with my mother-in-law. Seven months earlier, Zeldy had married Yitzchok Wasserman, and had moved to a community near Monsey, where Yitzchok had been living prior to their wedding.

My mother-in-law was eager to catch up with Zeldy and hear how she was adjusting to married life in the United States. During their conversation, Zeldy mentioned that she and her husband were seriously considering leaving their current residence and moving to Monsey, but it was not within their means to do so at the time. In fact, they were dismayed that they could not see an opportunity to make the move anytime in the near future.

My mother in-law suddenly had an inspiration. She felt the situation with Beatrice was less than ideal. It concerned her that my husband, who was already stretched thin, had to make a one-hour trip twice each weekend to drive Beatrice to and from our home. She suggested that Zeldy and her husband move into our house to run the household and take care of our children. For Zeldy and Yitzchok, it was a good opportunity to start out in Monsey rent free with almost no living expenses. At the same time, my husband offered to pay them what he had been paying Beatrice.

STRUGGLE TO THE SUMMIT

As my mother-in-law had expected, the Wassermans were excited about the proposition and accepted almost immediately. It seemed to be the perfect solution for our situation.

Within a couple of weeks, the Wassermans moved in with the Ehrmanns, to allow our children to adjust to them, while Beatrice remained for a few days. Afterwards, Beatrice parted on good terms, telling my husband, "If you ever need my help in the future, don't hesitate to call me."

The Wassermans planned to stay with the children at the Ehrmanns house until after Pesach and then move back into my house with them. In the meantime, my husband helped them move their furniture and other possessions from their original apartment into our house.

Shortly before these arrangements were made, about two and a half weeks after I arrived at Scenic View, Jewish communities worldwide celebrated the joyous *yom tov* of Purim. For me, it was a day that I will never forget. I was still experiencing numbness, fatigue, spinning and paresis, and I simply felt awful. My husband came on *Purim* night with someone to *lein* the *megillah*. I was sitting in the wheelchair at the time, counting the seconds for it to be finished. As soon as it was over, I collapsed into bed.

After my husband left, a group of high school girls came to sing and dance for me. I could hardly wait until they left, but I tried to smile, so they would think they were making me happy. I sighed with relief when they finally departed. Then my phone started ringing. Everyone wanted to let me know that they were thinking of me and to wish me *ah freilichin*

Pesach Approaches

Purim. Yeah, right! Each phone call took great effort. I cut each one short, hoping I was not offending anyone.

The following day was no easier. Though it was still Purim, I had to go to my regular therapy sessions. I had many more visitors than usual and received lots of *mishloach manos*. I could not open any myself, so they just made me feel worse, proving how incompetent I had become. Of course, had I not gotten any packages, I would have felt bad too, but I was so miserable, that they did not make me feel good either. Many people came and tried to cheer me up and give me *chizuk*, but I cried through most of these visits.

Later in the day, my husband brought my children. I cried some more. It was hard to feel a connection to them, so I felt terrible and could not stop crying. Only one thing gave me a reason to smile. The Ehrmanns had dressed my baby boy as a girl. He looked so cute and I did appreciate it.

For the Purim *seudah*, my brother Yosaif came with his wife, their two children, and my other brother Yaakov. They prepared a table in the lounge and brought along all the food. It was a beautiful *seuda*, but I did not have the stamina to join them for more than a half hour.

After Purim, I asked my husband to take home all the pretty packages that filled my room. Though I appreciated the thoughtfulness of the people who had sent them, I couldn't deal with a roomful of reminders of my inadequacies.

One evening, shortly after *Purim,* one of my visitors brought a bag full of *mishloach manos* leftovers. She wanted to get rid of them before Pesach and planned to leave the bag at the nurse's station. I noticed a box of milk chocolate among the items and asked her to leave it for me.

The following day, after I ate lunch, I asked my visitor to give me a chocolate, and I offered her one as well. I said a loud *brochah* and eagerly sunk my teeth into it. To my surprise, instead of tasting delicious, sweet chocolate, my teeth sank into hard, tasteless wax. It was not a box of chocolates at all! The package actually contained small candles that were designed to look and smell like truffles. Since I could not see well and always kept the lights off in my room, I had not realized that they were not actually chocolate!

Both of us burst into laughter. We found it so hilarious that it was worth the disappointment of not getting our expected treat. I laughed over the incident again and again. In fact, it kept me going for quite a while.

Before Pesach, I decided that I wanted to look prettier for *yom tov*. I asked my husband to bring me a pair of earrings, since I wanted to start wearing some jewelry again. It wasn't much, but at least I felt that I had done something special for *yom tov*.

Even though I could not be home for Pesach, I was comforted by the knowledge that my children were in good care. A friend bought them new clothes for *yom tov,* and they were nicely settled by the Ehrmanns with Zeldy and Yitzchok Wasserman. Meanwhile, my husband bought *matzoh* and other necessities, and Zehava Pearl cooked extra food, so that there would be enough for my husband and me as well. We were all set for *yom tov*.

Pesach Approaches

That year my husband performed *bedikas chametz* in three places: the apartment at the Ehrmanns, our house and my hospital room. On *erev* Pesach, he returned to my room lugging two coolers full of Pesach food. One had yogurt, cheese, cream cheese, butter, jam and other spreads for the *matzoh*. The other cooler had meat, fish, chicken and side dishes. He also brought a hot plate and timer to warm everything, as well as *matzoh*, grape juice, fresh vegetables, salt, drinks, plastic plates, cutlery, tablecloths and *bechers*. It was incredible how he thought of everything we might possibly need. We weren't lacking anything. He even included an assortment of *Pesach* nosh, and an extra box of *matzoh*, to keep in my room for the duration of *Pesach*.

During the *sedarim*, I remained in bed while my husband sat on a chair beside me, with the hospital tray table set as the *seder* table. I managed to read the whole *haggadah*, drink the four cups and eat some *matzoh*, though less than the required amount. Considering my situation, our *seder* went exceptionally well. Though we read the *haggadah* rather quickly, we still finished quite late. When I couldn't stay up any longer, I went to sleep in a bed full of *matzoh* crumbs.

The first two days of Pesach were weekdays. I had my regular therapy schedule, and we ate the *yom tov seudos* afterwards. I did not have my usual entourage of visitors, so I played some games with my husband instead. The weather was beautiful, and we spent some time outside. In the afternoon, when my husband napped, I passed the time by sitting at the nurse's station and talking to other patients.

STRUGGLE TO THE SUMMIT

On *chol hamoed*, I again enjoyed my usual rotation of visitors. Unlike the other weeks, though, my husband brought supper and ate with me each night. The second days of Pesach were much like the first, except that my husband invited a single friend of his to join us. They both slept in the hospital's dorm, and we ate the *seudos* together in my room.

My husband's English birthday came out on *chol hamoed* that year. I usually did not do anything special for the occasion, since my husband is not into birthdays and does not appreciate the fuss. Nonetheless, this time I wanted to show him that I was still his wife and express appreciation for all he had been doing.

The hospital had a gift shop that sold many cards. I didn't have any money, so I borrowed some from one of my visitors and asked her to take me down there. I purchased a birthday card and wrote a message in it. It was difficult for me to write, but the words were legible enough. Besides, I knew it was the thought that counted. Indeed, when I presented the card to my husband, he was surprised and delighted. "At last I see myself getting my wife back!" he told me happily.

After Pesach, I finally felt up to leaving my room. I started eating all the Shabbos *seudos* in the lounge. I spent much time there, and called it my personal living and dining room. My sister Hadassa and her friend Blimi came most Shabbosos after Pesach, and with their company and the variety of food brought by my husband, Shabbos was quite enjoyable. Moreover, I was once even joined by my own Shabbos guest!

During my therapy sessions, I had met and befriended an eighty-one-year-old widow, who was recovering from a stroke. She came from a nearby Jewish community but was not religious. Her three sons lived too far away to visit, and she would cry to me about how lonely she was. I felt sorry for her and often asked some of my visitors to stop into her room on their way out. Once when my husband was with me for Shabbos, I asked if she would like to join us for our Shabbos meal. She was delighted and so was I. Who would have dreamed I would be *zocheh* to do *hachnassas orchim* in the hospital?

9
Sub-Acute Unit

With time, I made progress. My tolerance for bright light increased, and the spinning and tremors ceased. I was able to sit on the edge of the bed without immediately falling over, and my speech began to improve. The numbness on my left side remained only in my hand, foot and face, and I no longer felt lopsided when I sat. I began having more energy and stopped going to sleep so early. I was finally beginning to feel human again.

The burn on my thigh healed slowly. The plastic surgeon suggested that I eat a lot of protein to promote faster healing. Every morning Zehava Pearl prepared a protein drink and sent it with my first visitor for breakfast. As the feeling in my left side returned, the burn started to hurt me, though it never became too painful to bear. Later, it became itchy as it healed, which was another discomfort I had to learn to tolerate.

About three months after I had been burned, the site still oozed slightly, but the doctor declared that it was finally healed. He changed my prescription to a moisturizer cream twice a day and said that I did not have to keep it covered anymore.

My steroid dosage was slowly decreased, and I became less bloated. My blood pressure stabilized and my thinking cleared. I still cried all the time about my situation, but my real personality resurfaced, and I began faring much better overall.

As with all medical care these days, the insurance company dictates a patient's medical treatment and my situation was no different. After twelve or thirteen weeks, my insurance company informed me that they would not pay for my stay in acute rehabilitation any longer. I wasn't in a condition to go home yet, so it was agreed that coverage would continue for a sub-acute facility. Scenic View has a sub-acute unit on the first floor of the hospital, and I was to be discharged from 4A and then admitted there at the end of April.

I was apprehensive about the move. I was familiar with the nurses on 4A, and they knew my condition and routine. It had taken time until I had learned to adapt to my environment, and I was afraid of the unknown. The one change I looked forward to was working with a new group of therapists. Each therapist has his or her own method, and I looked forward to hearing a fresh perspective.

I was not able to get a private room in the sub-acute unit, since single rooms were reserved for infectious patients. At first I was unhappy about sharing a room, but after a

Sub-Acute Unit

couple of days, I realized that I actually enjoyed my new surroundings. I was assigned the bed near the door and had my own sink in the corner. I had a little less space than in my previous room, but it was adequate. My room was located right near the nurse's station, and since there were always people walking by, I no longer felt so isolated. My roommate was an elderly woman who had broken her femur and her ankle when she was run over in a car accident. Though she was on the quiet side, she was pleasant company.

The first night that I was in sub-acute, when the nurse helped me change for the night, she pulled my skirt down and grazed the tender new skin that had grown over my burn. This caused excruciating pain, and I asked the nurse to put a bandage on it to protect it from happening again.

After that incident, I developed new blisters on the burn, and the doctor prescribed an antibiotic ointment to be applied twice a day. Every time the blisters healed, new ones would form. It continued like this until at least a month after I returned home.

In this new unit, the nurses were stricter about visiting hours and did not allow anyone to come before eleven in the morning to help me with my breakfast. I was faring much better by then and only needed someone to set up my food. One of the nurse's aides helped me with that, so I was able to eat breakfast on my own.

Since I was off the steroid medication, my eyesight improved. I still had double vision, but I was able to see clearly with one eye at a time. My husband had been in touch with Dr. Schick, and he strongly recommended that I wear an eye patch, explaining that it would also reduce my stress. I began wearing a patch and alternated eyes each day. As a result, I was able to focus and enjoy reading again. I had a couple of books I received as gifts, and once I saw how much I enjoyed reading, a friend brought some borrowed books for me. I was not able to hold a book, but I had to sit up and read as it lay on a table. With my improved tolerance for sitting, I was able to sit and read for hours on end.

In the sub acute unit, they showered the patients every other day. I had my showers with the help of an aide on Sunday, Tuesday and Friday. It was nice to have my hair washed a little more often than during the previous three months. On the other days, they expected me to wash up on my own, either in bed with a basin of water or sitting in front of the sink.

The first time they expected me to do this myself; the nurse's aide helped me into the wheelchair and brought me to the sink. She gave me disposable washcloths and my body soap and then walked out of the room. The sink was too high for me to reach properly. I was also uncoordinated and could not move well. I thought that this was a ridiculous way to wash and that it was unfair and outrageous that they expected me to do this on my own. I was so frustrated that I became hysterical and started crying. I told the aide that I could not wash up on my own. The nurses were not too sympathetic, but they soon realized that I really did need assistance.

My therapy routine in sub-acute was much less intense than on 4A. Each day I had only one half-hour session of occupational therapy and one half-hour session of physical therapy, which was devoted to working on my walking. I

Sub-Acute Unit

also spent an additional fifteen minutes on leg exercises and fifteen minutes on a Nu-step machine. This machine is similar to a stepper, but it has a seat and works the arms at the same time. I started doing ten minutes at a low level and increased to fifteen minutes at a higher level after only a few days.

My new occupational therapist gave me a sock aid to make it easier for me to put on my own socks and buttonhole tool, which is like a large needle threader, to make it easier to close buttons. These tools were efficient, but I had no intention of using them. In my opinion, these gadgets were designed for people who were much more functional and, by using these tools, were able to dress independently. I still needed someone to put my socks on the sock aid and bring it to me. I also needed someone to help me put on my shirt and hand me the buttonhole tool. I knew that I was only temporarily disabled, and I resented having someone stand by my side and watch me struggle needlessly when they could do the task much more quickly and efficiently.

Despite this, I liked the new therapists. The whole atmosphere in sub acute was much more relaxed. The unit was located on the ground floor and had easy access to the outdoors. The weather was warming up as it was already May, and I was finally feeling well enough to appreciate the beautiful view overlooking the Hudson River.

Though I was sleeping much better by now, I was still taking a sleeping pill each night. I wanted to begin weaning myself off it, so I asked the doctor to cut my dosage in half. Fortunately, I still slept just as well, but I was afraid to stop the medication altogether for fear of not being able to sleep. I planned to stay on the medication until I went home.

I still wrote every day in my notebook, but I wanted additional ways to practice my handwriting. I asked my husband to bring me our Boggle game from home and I started playing by myself. I had always enjoyed Boggle and this kept me quite busy while improving my writing skills too.

During my stay in the sub-acute unit, my hair suddenly started to fall out. I had hair all over my pillow and on the floor and my hairbrush had to be cleaned twice each time I used it. My hair became thin and straggly. I asked the doctor about this, and she said that this often occurs after a big trauma. She reassured me that it was only temporary.

I had been covering my hair with a snood that I had from before my surgery. By this time, it had stretched out and constantly slid back. I became terribly upset about this since I could not readjust it myself. I felt so incapable that I could not even keep my hair covered properly. Once when this happened I started crying out of sheer frustration. Just then, a woman from Bikur Cholim came to bring me lunch. When I explained why I was so upset, she told me that she used snap clips to keep her snood in place. She took off her own clips and gave them to me. They worked wonderfully and from then on my snood stayed in place. It was such a simple gesture, but it made me feel so much better.

By this time, I had started keeping myself occupied with various activities. I did not watch TV anymore and had fewer visitors. I was not as desperate for company as before, since I no longer felt as helpless and alone and was busy until lunch with occupational therapy and leg exercise sessions. I had a

Sub-Acute Unit

visitor each day for lunch, and she would stay until one thirty or two o'clock. After she left, I usually relaxed in bed and watched a video. The hospital had a VCR that they wheeled into my room, and together with my roommate, I watched a video from the hospital's large lending library.

At three thirty, I had my physical therapy session and after that I usually read until another visitor brought supper at five o'clock. She stayed while I ate, and when I was finished, we would either go outside, play games or just chat.

Since I had been forced into inactivity for so long, I became eager to do something productive with my time. In the past, I had enjoyed assembling jigsaw puzzles, and I'd often done one thousand piece puzzles in about a week's time. I decided to try doing a jigsaw puzzle again and asked a friend to send me one.

My friend bought a beautiful thousand-piece puzzle that was made out of a special foam material called Perfa-lock. It was easier for me to grasp and the pieces did not fall apart like conventional cardboard puzzles. I asked someone else to bring me two poster boards, and I assembled the puzzle on them. I worked on and kept my puzzle in the dining room, which had cabinets and a long counter on one side of the room. I kept the puzzle on the counter and put a sign on top that read, "Private. Do not touch."

I used only my right hand to work on the puzzle. My visitors helped me sort and pick out the pieces I needed. When the puzzle was more than halfway complete, someone messed it up and put it back in the box. I was quite disappointed, but in a way, I was relieved. I had already finished the easier parts of the puzzle; what remained were the challenging pieces, which I was afraid I wouldn't be able to complete.

Even though I did not eat the hospital dinners, I still had to fill out the menu for breakfast and drinks. I had always asked one of my visitors to fill out the menu for me, but after I moved to sub acute, I tried to manage myself. Though my writing was sloppy, it was legible enough. I felt quite accomplished being able to complete this simple task on my own.

I always tried to use some of my free time to do therapy on my own. I asked my husband to buy a Rubik's cube, figuring it would be good for my hands. I played with the cube when I was in bed or when I was bored. I also asked Yisroel to bring my baby's snap beads toy, and I practiced taking them apart and putting them together. I asked for a negel vasser cup with two handles, so I could wash my hands on my own. This was good practice as well, and I was able to do it even though my left hand was still quite clumsy. Another thing I requested was a beach ball. It was an inexpensive item that allowed for an interactive therapy activity, as I used it to play catch with some of my visitors. I did not have too much storage space in my room, otherwise I would have asked for many more items.

Though I had finished taking the steroid medication when I was still in 4A, I continued receiving medication to lower my blood pressure. Since my blood pressure had returned to normal, I asked the doctor why I still needed it. She said that she would write a note for the nurse to discontinue the medication. That night, the nurse came to give me medication as usual.

Sub-Acute Unit

"Did you see the note left by the doctor in my chart?" I asked her.

The nurse admitted that she hadn't even glanced at my chart. Once again, I was reminded of the importance of remaining alert and being involved in my own care.

Though I wasn't depressed anymore, I still cried frequently. I cried whenever I thought of or talked about my children, but if I tried not to think about them, I felt like an uncaring mother. I also cried whenever someone commented on my improvement, since I felt that my progress was too slow. During therapy, when just walking across the room would completely wipe me out, I would say, "It's so hard! I feel as though I'm climbing a mountain!" and then burst into tears as I recognized how dire my condition truly was.

My left hand had a sensory problem, and it was stressful for me to touch anything with it. Any contact to my fingers would cause itching and a strange sensation. I couldn't stand the feeling. I usually sat with my left hand on my lap with my palm facing upwards. I could not even take the feeling of my fingers touching my skirt.

My occupational therapist told me that this was not a normal position for my hand and insisted that I keep my palm down. To desensitize my hand, she had me place it inside a Fluido machine. This machine blew around ground up cornhusks to help sensitive skin get used to contact. I put my hand in the Fluido for fifteen minutes every day, and touch became more tolerable afterwards. I was finally able to start keeping my hand in a normal position.

My husband brought a friend's old laptop computer to the hospital for me. He had put all the family pictures from my home computer on it, and I had a constant slide show of my children and home. I enjoyed this immensely, but it also made me even more homesick. The last time I had seen my children was when my husband had brought them on erev Pesach. I had cried throughout the entire visit, and my husband felt it was best not to bring them anymore.

In addition to providing photos from home, the laptop computer also helped me pass the time after visiting hours. My husband brought me a computer table on wheels that rose up and had an adjustable slant, enabling me to watch DVDs while I was in my bed at night. Once someone set up this table at a good angle, I was able to control the computer myself. Since my roommate was always watching TV and the speakers were near her bed, the sound from the DVD did not disturb her.

I watched DVDs for a short while but soon found that I did not enjoy them so much. By the time I was in bed, I had already washed my face for the night and removed my patch. I had to strain to keep one eye closed, since my vision was double when both eyes were open.

I soon discovered another nighttime activity. I had a big tape recorder that my husband brought me when I first came to the hospital. I had a number of cassette tapes of various lectures that people had brought, but it had been too hard for me to use the tape recorder previously. Now, I started asking my last visitor of the day to set the tape recorder on the tray table right next to my bed. Once I was in bed, I asked the

Sub-Acute Unit

nurse to position it for me over the bed. This way I was able to control the buttons and listen to the tape.

By now, the clock had been changed to daylight savings time, and Shabbos ended late. Hadassa usually came with her friend, and as we had done on unit 4A, we used the lounge to eat and play games. Since the weather was warm and I was on the ground level, we spent part of the long Shabbos afternoon outside. If not for my condition, it would have felt as if we were at a vacation resort. We once even ate *shalosh seudos* outside and it was quite enjoyable.

For months now, my husband had regularly been packing large coolers with Shabbos or *yom tov* food. While this had always been a time-consuming and difficult task, he did it diligently without complaint. He did not only include the basic Shabbos foods, but dips and other extras as well.

Now, as Shavuos approached, my husband planned to come with the same friend who had accompanied him during the last days of Pesach. He again packed full menus for all the meals into a large cooler on wheels. Among the contents was a container of salty, oily herring. After arriving at Scenic View, he noticed that the container had cracked and smelly fish oil had leaked over all the contents. The odor was strong and quickly spreading throughout the ward.

This was the last straw for him. "That's it!" he exclaimed, surveying the mess. "I can't take this anymore! You are coming home!"

Watching from my wheelchair, I found the episode comical and could not stop laughing. If it had been up to me, there never would have been herring there in the first place. My husband had no choice but to clean up the greasy mess all on his own. Astoundingly, though, his words turned out to be prophetic.

10
Home at Last

The day after Shavuos we had a meeting about my discharge schedule with the hospital social worker. Shavuos was on Friday and Shabbos, and, believing that I was ready to go home, they set my discharge date for the following Friday. In fact, as my husband had hoped, he never had to pack that dreaded cooler again!

My husband was left with the burden of finding a full-time aide who would assist me with my basic needs. We had only a few days to find someone, and he didn't know where to start looking. Zehava Pearl came to the rescue again. Through the grapevine, she found a Brazilian woman named Marcia who seemed suitable for the job. My husband drove her down to the hospital for training on how to walk with me and help me transfer to and from the wheelchair.

When my husband introduced me to Marcia, a broad, homely woman of about forty, I immediately felt comfortable with her. She seemed like the take-charge type, which was exactly what I needed then. In addition to preparing Marcia to assist me, my physical therapist ordered some items that I would need at home: a wheelchair, a walker, a wide base quad cane and a shower chair.

I was both eager and apprehensive about going home. My bedroom is on the second floor, and I worried whether I would be able to climb the steps. My balance was impaired, and I could not go to the bathroom without assistance. My husband tried to reassure me, but I could not even explain all my fears. I was also anxious to finally see my children, but I was nervous about how they would react to me. I knew that Zeldy and Yitzchok Wasserman had become part of my household, and I wondered how I would adjust to having another couple living with us. I was afraid my house would feel different, and I wanted to come home to the home I knew.

At around nine thirty on Friday morning, my husband came to the hospital with Marcia and packed up all my things. I had been there for several months and had quite an accumulation of belongings. My physical therapist came out to teach me how to get in and out of the car. Afterwards, my husband loaded everything up, and we were ready to go. I said goodbye to the staff and other patients, and with a sense of relief, I left the place that had felt like a prison for four long months.

I was so nervous during the ride home that I felt slightly carsick. I had not been inside a moving vehicle for a long time, and I had never liked being a passenger. I cried a little on the way and felt very anxious. It was strange to be on

Home at Last

the road and to see cars and houses. It felt surreal when we arrived at our street and turned onto our driveway.

Our garage is attached to the house and a doorway leads directly into the kitchen, so there were no steps for me to deal with. We pulled into the garage and my husband unloaded my wheelchair and helped me into it. He wheeled me into the house. I was overwhelmed by emotion and burst into tears. Luckily, my children were napping. I was not ready to see them just yet.

My husband had borrowed a recliner from someone, and he helped me into it. We had a glider and couch, but neither would have worked for me. The couch was too low for me to stand up from, and the glider moved around, making it impractical for me transfer in and out of it. A recliner was the perfect solution, and it allowed me to avoid sitting in the uncomfortable wheelchair all day.

When I was settled in the recliner, my children woke up from their naps. Libby, who was almost two, was shy and stayed at the other side of the room. Shloimy, who was ten months old, did not remember me at all.

Both of them had grown and changed so much. Though I had resolved not to cry in front of Libby, I became emotional and could not hold back the tears. To my dismay, she became scared and started crying too.

When things settled down, Zeldy cooked a pot of pasta and brought me some to eat. Libby warmed up to me and came to help herself from my bowl. This made me feel a little better, but I still did not feel as though I was her mother yet.

When I had to use the bathroom, we realized that the wheelchair did not fit through the bathroom door. I still could not stand on my own, and Marcia had to walk with me inside. The toilet posed additional challenges, since those in the hospital were higher and easier for me to use. Despite all the difficulties, we managed to get over that hurdle. I calmed down as I realized that other things would somehow work out too.

Since it was early summer, we had plenty of time until Shabbos. Marcia and my husband carried my things up to my bedroom and unpacked for me. Later, my husband drove Marcia home for the weekend. He would be the only one helping me until Sunday.

When it was time for candle lighting, I was wheeled over to the candles to *bentch licht*. My hand was unsteady, and since I was seeing from only one eye, my depth perception was off. It was hard for me to tell exactly where the wick was, and it took a few tries until the candles were lit. I did not stand up or cover my eyes, since balancing on my feet and lifting my hands were too difficult. The whole experience was extremely emotional, especially since I had not lit Shabbos candles in over four months.

My husband *davened* at home, since he was concerned that I might need his help. When Yitzchok Wasserman came home from *shul*, my husband wheeled me to the dining room table. It was too difficult to get to the sink for *netilas yadayim*, so he washed my hands with a cup and bowl. The food tasted like my own, since Zeldy had asked me for instructions on how to cook everything. It felt strange but good to be at home at my own Shabbos table.

Home at Last

It was late by the time the *seudah* was over. I was tired and wanted to go straight to bed. Going upstairs was not easy. I went up sideways, holding onto the railing with both hands. My husband followed right behind me. Since I wore a brace on my left foot that held my ankle in a fixed position, I was unable to bend it. I stepped up onto each next step with my right foot and then brought my left one up behind it. When we reached the landing, my husband supported me as I made my way into our bedroom.

The upstairs bathroom provided more of a challenge since it is smaller than the one downstairs. My husband had wisely turned the door around before I came home so that it opened outward instead of inward. Without this change, the door would have gotten in the way, making things even more difficult.

After getting ready to go to sleep, I finally found myself in my own bed again. I was used to the hospital mattress, which felt different and was able to recline. It was strange to be on a flat bed with a thick quilt again.

For the first time in a long while, I did not take a sleeping pill. Fortunately, I still managed to fall asleep before long. I woke up once during the night and then again early the next morning. This time, I could not fall back asleep. My husband helped me get dressed and assisted me down the stairs to the kitchen. After giving me something to eat, he helped me into the recliner.

Zeldy was already downstairs with the children at the time. I was still tired and kept yawning as I tried to read a book. Libby, who was playing on the floor, watched me. "Mommy, are you tired?" she asked. "Do you need a blanket?"

She was so sweet, and I could not believe how articulate she was. I started dozing off, but every so often I would open my eyes. Each time, Libby exclaimed, "Hello, Mommy!"

She was so precious, and I had missed out so much of her growing up. Throughout the day, I enjoyed watching the children and seeing how much they had changed.

Shabbos and Sunday passed relatively smoothly. On Sunday evening, my husband picked up Marcia. She gave me my first shower at home. I had worried about this as well, but it worked out in the end.

During my first week at home, there wasn't much for me to do. I wouldn't start outpatient therapy until the following Thursday, so I could not set up a routine yet.

After only a few days at home, my right knee started aching. I realized that it bore most of my body weight each time I stood up. In the hospital, I had to stand only during therapy, when I went to use the bathroom or when I was transferred to my bed. At home, I also went up and down stairs and walked from the landing to my bedroom each day. Since my left leg was much weaker, I automatically put my weight into my right leg. As a result, my right knee carried most of the burden and became strained. It was so tender that I was concerned I had developed a chronic problem. From then on, I tried to consciously shift my weight into my left leg and the pain gradually diminished.

I cried a lot during my first few days at home. Zeldy updated me on my children's development and told me how they had been during the past few months. Each story triggered a new flood of tears. From all that she related, I realized that Libby had suffered from my absence. Shloimy, who was younger, was unaffected and well adjusted. I was happy to see that my children liked Zeldy and Yitzchok. Both treated them as if they were their own children, giving them lots of love and attention. I admit that I felt a bit jealous, but I tried hard to push the feeling away.

Even though she hadn't seen me in such a long time, Libby was truly happy to have me home. She seemed to understand my limitations and just accepted me the way I was. She enjoyed merely sitting on my lap when I was on the recliner. When she hurt herself, she wanted me to kiss the booboo. When she hurt herself on her knee or another place that was out of my reach, I would kiss her hand and tell her to put the kiss on the booboo. This satisfied her.

Libby was very protective of my things. Yitzchok once sat down on my wheelchair and Libby looked at him indignantly. "Its Mommy's chair! GET OFF!" she ordered

When Libby once spotted the ugly mark from the burn on my thigh, she asked me what it was. "It's a booboo that Mommy got," I told her.

"I'm gonna kiss it, and it will get all better," she replied.

She was so sweet and innocent and truly believed a kiss could heal booboos.

Shloimy was ten months old and a cheerful, active little boy. When I left him, he had been an infant who could not do much, but now he was crawling around and babbling constantly. He had turned into quite a personality.

From the day I came home, Libby insisted that only Mommy could give her a bottle. Zeldy would prepare it and give it to me, and I would hand it to Libby. Only then was she happy. In truth, it gave me a warm feeling too. Even though I wasn't actually doing anything, it made me feel like a mother to my child.

At first, Libby called my cane a hanger, because the handle resembled the top of a hanger. Later, she started treating it as if it were a living being. She would lie it down on the floor and cover it with a blanket. "It's going to sleep," she would tell me quietly. Another time she said, "The cane has a booboo and needs to go to the doctor."

Libby also fed the cane her bottle, as she did her dolls. The cane had a small hole on the handle that she called the mouth. She was very accepting of my cane as if it was part of the family.

Zeldy was incredibly sweet and sensitive and tried to make me feel in charge of the household chores. She would ask me what to make for supper, what to feed Shloimy or when to put him in for a nap. While I appreciated her thoughtfulness, I often had no idea how to respond to these questions. "You know better than me," I would tell her.

It took some time, but I slowly learned how to run my house again. At first Zeldy wrote all the shopping lists and called the grocery to place the orders. After a few weeks, I started planning menus, making grocery lists and calling in the orders myself.

My husband, who had missed my cooking, was happy to have "my" food again. Though I did not actually cook, Zeldy followed my instructions and everything came out like when I had prepared it.

Home at Last

I began outpatient therapy in Scenic View twice a week, on Tuesday and Thursday afternoons. I had one hour of occupational therapy and one hour of physical therapy each time. Marcia drove me in our minivan, and I arrived back home exhausted at around five o'clock. Because I disliked traveling and the sessions were so exhausting, I did not enjoy these bi-weekly therapy outings.

Once during my session of OT, my therapist gave me a printout of arm exercises and showed me how to do them at home. She put a mirror in front of me so I could see what I was doing. One exercise required me to stretch both arms straight out and then lift them up over my head. My left arm was still weak and I could not straighten my elbow. When I saw myself in the mirror and realized how uncoordinated I appeared, I burst into tears. It was very difficult for me to see myself like that.

In addition to my outpatient therapy sessions, I also tried doing my own therapies at home, such as stringing beads, putting coins into a piggy bank and other activities that enhanced my fine motor skills. I continued writing in my notebook every day and my writing skills improved with time. One activity that I could not manage was peeling potatoes. Each time I tried, the potato would slip out of my left hand.

I also purchased various items to use for therapy at home, including a game of Chinese checkers, a package of clothespins, a word search book, a shoe tying puzzle, some adult coloring books and a box of colored pencils. My goal was to do as much therapy as I could on my own.

Besides working on my fine motor skills, I made sure to focus on practicing walking. I was able to walk a full loop in my house, since the kitchen, living room and two hallways connected. I walked twice around this loop two times each day. Marcia walked with me, with one hand on my left hip and the other on my right shoulder to help me balance. As my balance improved, I walked while wearing a gait belt, which is a wide belt that is worn around the waist. By holding onto it lightly from behind, an aide can prevent falls if the patient loses her balance.

I also started working on improving my endurance for standing. I began by standing at the kitchen table for five minutes a day. It was not easy at first, and I was quite shaky. I was not used to having my body weight in my feet. My body felt like heavy lead. I slowly increased my standing time and became more stable. Having weight in my feet did not feel normal for a long time, but eventually I stopped noticing it.

I primarily walked with a quad cane, but sometimes I used a walker to practice walking more continuously. When I used the cane, I first put it forward and then moved my left foot and finally my right. I had to pause between each step to move the cane. With the walker, I was able to keep pushing forward, putting one foot in front of the other without pausing between steps.

Most people take the normal motions involved in walking for granted, but I had to relearn minor details. For example, when walking with the cane, my right foot simply met the left one with each step I took. Later, when I practiced walking continuously, my therapist helped me learn to take normal size steps and put my right foot past my left foot. I had to consciously do this with each step until it came naturally.

Home at Last

My therapist also focused on teaching me to move my cane and left foot simultaneously, so that my walking should not be done in three steps. Since my left leg was so weak, I had to lean on the cane when I picked up my right foot to take a step. When I moved my left leg and supported myself on my right foot, I was able to learn to move my cane at the same time. With this new walking pattern, I was able to walk more continuously with my cane and stop using the bulky walker.

As I practiced, I was amazed at all the minute details I had to focus on. I looked around and marveled at all the people walking around without giving any thought to balance or to where to place their feet.

To keep my mind stimulated, I started working on a new 1000 piece jigsaw puzzle. I had never completed the one in the hospital. I had assumed some pieces were lost when it was messed up. Now, I started a new one on my dining room table and spent many hours working on it each day. The puzzle served as a great distraction and over the next several months, I finished five jigsaw puzzles.

Each day, Marcia insisted that I go upstairs at seven thirty in the evening. My bedtime routine took about an hour and Marcia wanted to go to bed by nine o'clock. I felt stifled by this, but I cooperated with her because I wanted her to be happy.

Marcia slept in our extra bedroom, and during the night, my husband assisted me when necessary. At eight o'clock in the morning, Marcia would resume her caretaking role and knock on my door to help me start my day.

Shortly after I came home, I organized my clothes closet with Marcia. All the clothes I could wear were hung together, while those that were out of season or the wrong size were pushed to one side. I had been wearing a plain black skirt and button down shirt every day for four months and it was nice to wear some of my other clothes again.

As I organized myself, I wrote a list of household items and toiletries that I could not order from the grocery store. I decided to go to Wal-Mart to buy them. Zeldy had to come along, since I needed one person to push me in the wheelchair and another to push the shopping cart. Libby sat on my lap in the wheelchair, and Shloimy sat in the shopping cart. I felt self-conscious going out in public in a wheelchair, but I came to terms with it before long. It dispirited me terribly, though, that I was sitting too low and far from the shelves to be able to see the merchandise properly. While I was happy to be out shopping again, I could not shake the feeling of despair and incompetence, as I realized that I could not even shop like a normal customer.

Despite my despondency regarding my situation, it felt wonderful to be out and about. We began making regular shopping trips, visiting the local Shoprite, Wal-Mart and Shopper's Haven, a Jewish shopping mall with a large kosher supermarket.

One week I decided that it would be nice to bake *challos*. Zeldy followed my recipe to prepare the dough and I braided them at the kitchen table. I wore gloves, since I did not want to deal with dough stuck under my fingernails. I taught Zeldy how to form six-braid *challos*. My left hand worked well enough for the *challos* to come out looking quite nice.

Home at Last

I was happy to finally be doing something productive. It was an activity we both enjoyed, so we continued baking *challos* every week.

Other than braiding the *challos*, I was rarely involved in any food preparation. Among the few tasks I was able to do were cutting off the ends of green beans and chopping up vegetables for a salad on Shabbos. One week, though, I cut my finger pretty badly, so I stopped preparing the salad.

A couple of weeks after I came home, I started to *daven* each morning. It was not easy at first. Speaking was still exhausting. I pronounced each word slowly and often stumbled on some of them. With time, it became easier. I think *davening* was one of the best speech therapies for me. My speech remained slightly stilted for some time, and though I was told that it was fine, I knew it sounded a bit labored.

In July, a couple of months after I came home, one of my younger brothers became engaged to a girl from Flatbush. The *vort* was in Brooklyn at a house with a disabled member in the family. I knew that there would be a ramp and accessible bathroom, so I decided to attend. It would be my first public appearance since the surgery.

A neighbor came over to put on my makeup and shaitel. I wore an outfit I had bought the previous summer for my brother's *bar mitzvah,* which had been just five weeks after Shloimy was born. The outfit was a comfortable black three piece, and it looked nice and suited me well.

Though we had a smooth drive, I felt uncomfortable once I arrived at the *vort*. The place was crowded, and I had a perfect view of everyone's midsection from the wheelchair. With so many people around, I was also embarrassed when my husband helped me to the bathroom. My speech was still labored and making conversation was exhausting. Even though everyone was happy to see me, I just wanted to go home. We stayed for about half an hour and then left.

With time, I settled into a nice routine at home. I loved being with my children, and it gave me immense pleasure to watch them play. However, some episodes were especially hard for me. Once, for example, Shloimy was teething badly and crying incessantly. Nothing Zeldy did calmed him. I asked her to put him on my lap, but he would not come to me, since he did not know me as his mother. I felt so inadequate as I sat there unable to do anything for my baby, and I burst into tears.

Another time Libby refused to take a bath. She just cried and cried without telling anyone what was wrong. I asked Zeldy to bring her to me and put her on my lap. I tried talking to her and calming her down, but that did not help either. In the end, it became too late for a bath, and she went straight to bed.

These occurrences showed me how much my children needed me to get better and become fully functional again. Indeed, I was doing everything within my power to accelerate the process.

Home at Last

Zeldy remembers:

When Mrs. Zucker from England first broached the idea of having my husband and I move into Rivkah's home, I immediately recognized that this was a wonderful opportunity – mamash min hashamayim. First of all, I was extremely grateful to the Zuckers for all they had done for me in the past and now was my chance to express hakaros hatov to them. In addition, my husband and I hoped that by accepting the position we would be able to recognize our dream of eventually moving into our own residence in Monsey.

They say that if you want to teach someone how to swim, throw the person into water. In a way, that's how it was with me. I was newly married at the time and quite inexperienced in running a home, preparing meals and caring for children. When I was suddenly thrust into this role, it was hard for me at first, but I learned to do things more quickly than I had ever imagined possible. Once Rivkah came home from Scenic View, I learned even more, and I gained tremendously as we did various activities together. She gave me many housekeeping tips and even taught me how to braid challos.

While she guided me during chores that we did together, Rivkah never criticized how I did things that I took care of myself. I knew that she is an extremely organized and efficient person and her home had always been immaculate. Though I tried my best, I am sure that I often did not do things to her complete satisfaction. It must have been difficult for her to watch someone else do her job in a much less competent manner. Nonetheless, she never said a word to me about anything. I marveled at her strength of character and her ability to accept her situation.

One of the more challenging aspects of my job was dealing with Libby's tantrums. It was clear that she was going through a very difficult time, since she was old enough to remember how her mother had once been. She was at an age when most children are difficult and obstinate, but in her case, she truly had good reason to act out. Quite often, I felt unsure whether the right thing was to discipline her or show her love.

It was much easier for me to deal with Shloimy. He was too young to miss his mother and immediately became very attached to me. He was an adorable, outgoing baby, and we bonded really well. I loved him so much that when I was at the end of my first pregnancy, I worried whether I would be able to love my own child as much as I loved Shloimy. Of course, I was still unaware of the overwhelming, instinctive maternal love one feels after the birth of a child.

After my baby was born, many visitors commented that I handled my baby so capably and did not look like a first-time mother. "Well, I am not really a first time mother," I'd reply. I had become so attached to Rivkah's children that I actually felt that I was already a mother.

While I was busy taking care of the house, Rivkah devoted herself completely to improving her function. I was amazed at her fighting spirit. She never rested for long and always looked for new activities and therapies to do. She went for outpatient therapy, did exercises at home and invited people to play games with her. She also made sure to eat healthy foods and take care of herself properly. Most people in her situation would probably lie despondently in bed for days on end, but her determination to recover was unbelievable. It was an inspiration for those around her to watch how hard she worked and how cheerful she usually was, despite her trials and tribulations.

One day, Rivkah pointed to a patch of soil in her yard. "See that? That's my vegetable garden," she told me. "One day I will plant cucumbers and tomatoes again." It seemed like an unrealistic goal when she said it. Some time later, though, she bought large flowerpots. She still cannot plant vegetables in the ground, but she figured she could plant some on her patio. Believe it or not, I have already tasted the vegetables she has grown!

Though I worked incredibly hard during my time in Rivkah's house, when I look back to that period in my life, I only recall pleasant memories. Rivkah and her husband are such wonderful people that, amazingly enough, though my husband and I spent more than six months in their home, there was never any friction between us. We all have our idiosyncrasies, but we managed to get along and make the best of a challenging situation. Personally, I gained so much from my time with the Zuckers. I learned valuable life lessons about running a home and facing challenges that will remain with me always.

11
More Adjustments

After some time, I became increasingly annoyed with Marcia's attitude. At first, I had been impressed with her take-charge manner, but after a while it seemed that she wanted to take complete control of my life.

Marcia acted as if I were her charge. She kept reminding me to do the exercises that the therapists had suggested and to wash my face with my left hand instead of my right. Whenever she watched me doing leg exercises, she stood over me and insisted on telling me the "right way" to do them. In addition, she typed up a list of all the different exercises my therapists had recommended. Acting like my teacher, she marked off each one as I did it and wrote progress notes about me. When she returned each Sunday, Marcia asked what I had done over the weekend, so that she could record it and write everything down.

Once, as she was interrogating me about my activities, I exclaimed in exasperation, "Do you also want to know how many times I blew my nose and went to the bathroom?"

Marcia also argued over issues relating to running my household. For example, when I wanted to buy a generic brand of window cleaner, Marcia insisted that only Windex would work for her. Similarly, she repeatedly demanded that I buy air fresheners for the bathroom, even though I explained that the chemicals are unhealthy and give me headaches. She also wanted to wash my leather sneakers in the washing machine, arguing with me when I said that they were not washable.

These incidents were extremely upsetting. True, I was sitting in a wheelchair and dependent on those around me, but this did not mean that I could no longer be in charge of my own life. I resented having someone tell me what to do.

If these issues were not enough to cause friction, Marcia soon began shirking and complaining about her responsibilities. She claimed that lifting the wheelchair in and out of the car was hurting her back. Though she hinted for us to pay for her chiropractic visits, we ignored the insinuations. When I asked her to vacuum once, she *kvetched*, "Oh, please do not ask me to do that. My back hurts."

Marcia liked to take walks outside after dinner in the evening. I did not mind, as long as she told me her intentions and did not just disappear. One evening after supper, I was working on my puzzle when I wanted to use the bathroom. For forty-five minutes, I kept calling for Marcia, but she was nowhere in sight. Finally, she reappeared. She had gone outside for a walk without telling me beforehand.

More Adjustments

Marcia found herself a chiropractor in the neighborhood and started to see him a couple of times a week. Once when we returned from therapy, I asked her to help me to the bathroom. Marcia told me that she had to rush to the chiropractor. They were about to close and were just waiting for her. She asked me to wait until she came back. I was able to wait and did not make a fuss about it, but I thought it was extremely insensitive of her.

We had hired Marcia to help me when necessary, but I repeatedly found myself without assistance when I needed it.

On top of all this, Marcia had issues with kosher food and complained about the food restrictions in our home. Once Zeldy cooked pasta in a dairy pot and fried onions for something else in a meat pot. Marcia helped herself to some fried onions to eat together with her pasta on a dairy plate. Zeldy told her to use a disposable plate if she wanted to eat it together. Marcia became insulted, threw her food in the garbage and went upstairs to her room. She sulked for the rest of the day and refused to eat anything else.

At first, I just gritted my teeth whenever I became upset and tried to act nicely. As these incidents increased in frequency, my resentment towards her grew and her mere presence irked me.

One evening there was an emergency at my husband's workplace, and he informed us that he would have to work through most of the night. Since he usually assisted me to the bathroom in middle of the night, he gave Marcia a cell phone and arranged that I would call her when I needed her. Several hours after I went to sleep, I awoke and needed her assistance. I kept calling the cell phone, but Marcia did not answer. In the end, I called my husband, who had to drop everything at work and rush home to help me. It took him about forty-five minutes to get home. Needless to say, we were incensed. It was the final straw for both of us, and we decided to let Marcia go.

As much as I resented Marcia, I was nervous about managing without her. I was extremely dependent on the help of others. She had already learned my routine and preferences for the way I liked things done. My husband tried to reassure me, but I was quite apprehensive about starting with someone new.

At the time, my mother in-law was visiting from England. My husband told Marcia that she would be staying to help me, since he could no longer afford to keep her. It was a nice way of letting her go without making her feel bad. When she left that last Friday, I felt such a sense of relief. I hadn't even realized how stifled I felt and just how much I missed my freedom.

During the following week, we interviewed several women for the position. Since my situation already caused enough aggravation, I wanted an aide who would not further frustrate me. It was important that I find someone who could provide the care I needed, while still allowing me to feel comfortable and in charge. Finally, after meeting three different people, we heard of someone who seemed like a good candidate.

In addition to his main job, my husband regularly fixed machines for a large local bakery, and he knew the Polish woman who worked at the counter there. One day he asked her if she could recommend someone who might be suitable to work as my aide. The woman suggested a young Polish

More Adjustments

girl named Kasia (pronounced Ka-sha). Kasia was a twenty-four-year-old college student who was visiting for a few months and living at the same boarding house. My husband arranged to pick her up for an interview at our house that same evening.

Kasia was thin, about five and a half feet tall, and she had long straight dark hair. She seemed intelligent and pleasant, and she spoke English fairly well. I liked her right away, and we hired her to begin working for us the following morning.

Kasia was a real pleasure. She cleaned the house well and helped Zeldy in the kitchen. She promptly learned my routine and helped me with my exercises. Unlike Marcia, Kasia didn't sleep in my home. She came in the morning and went home in the evening when my husband came home. She would help me with my bedtime routine, and I would then return downstairs in my robe before she left. I no longer had to be in bed by eight and was able to have visitors in the evening.

I decided to resume playing games for therapy, as I had done in the hospital. Zehava Pearl again arranged for visitors. This became my schedule every evening after Libby went to bed, from eight until nine o'clock. I called these nightly sessions my play dates, and they provided a much-needed social outlet.

As I played, I focused on specific areas. First I played a game while standing to increase my endurance; then I played a game using only my left hand; and finally, I played Boggle to improve my writing speed. Though my handwriting had drastically improved, I was still unable to write at a normal speed.

When I first came home from the hospital, my AFO brace was fixed at the ankle. It held my foot and ankle in an unmovable position. I felt restrained and disliked wearing it. I only put it on when I needed to walk. About six weeks after I came home, my physical therapist felt it was time to modify the brace. According to her instructions, the brace was cut and a hinge was added to allow for increased movement. Once my brace was articulated, I was able to move my ankle and started wearing it all the time.

About two months after I came home, my balance improved enough for me to be able to use the bathroom on my own. Even Zeldy was now able to help me walk to and from the bathroom. With this new development, I realized that if I could get to the bathroom on my own at night I would no longer have to wake my husband. To make this possible, I asked him to move my bed closer to the wall and put bars along the wall leading into the bathroom and to the toilet. Walking sideways, I was able to grip the bars and make my way to the bathroom. This new independence gave me a real sense of satisfaction.

As I continued making progress, my bedtime routine became easier, too. With experience, I learned to wear garments that closed in the front, allowing me to change on my own. I needed assistance going upstairs, but otherwise I managed to do almost everything independently.

Outpatient therapy ended after only two months, when my insurance no longer covered it. At that point, I knew that I had to take my therapy into my own hands. With my therapist's assistance, I ordered an arm pedal device; it was a machine I had used in therapy that I felt was crucial for my recovery.

More Adjustments

I used it every day at home. I also added an hour of game playing, from eleven to twelve each morning.

I wanted to practice walking, too, but I felt that my home was not the right venue for this. During the day, there were usually toys strewn across the floor. Additionally, the layout of the house inhibited me from covering a large distance in one stretch.

Fortunately, I found the perfect place to hold my own therapy sessions. The Shopper's Haven, a new local mall, had a large kosher supermarket on the first floor and a number of stores set around a large open square on the second. The mall was relatively quiet during certain hours of the day and it became my destination for daily walking exercises.

The open square provided a nice view of the supermarket's large, colorful produce aisle below, and Kasia accompanied me as I walked around it with my quad cane. I made three laps each day, sitting down for a break in my wheelchair after each one. I walked with the gait belt for security, though I had become more stable and did not lose my balance anymore. My walking improved from week to week, giving me much needed encouragement.

I soon began visiting the stores located on that floor following my exercise routine. I bought a robe for *yom tov* in the robe store and toys for my children at the toy store. I also shopped at the health and hosiery stores and enlarged my rings at the jewelry store.

Before going home, we frequently went to the supermarket downstairs. Though I still called in my weekly shopping order by phone, I preferred choosing some items myself. Kasia pushed me around, while I sat in the wheelchair with a basket on my lap. We were able to buy whatever fit inside. On one occasion, I wanted to make a larger grocery order, and we filled three baskets, bringing one at a time to the register when it filled up. After paying for everything, a worker brought everything out in a shopping cart for us. All in all, the mall was a most convenient place and I often joked that it had been built especially for me.

While still in therapy, my occupational therapist had suggested that I do eye exercises to cure my double vision. She recommended some exercises that would encourage both eyes to work together, but they did not work out well. I came up with another idea and asked my husband to buy a laser pointer. While lying in bed at night without my eye patch, I pointed the laser at the ceiling and followed the light with both eyes as I moved it back and forth, up and down and in large circles.

While I was able to do all these exercises on my own, my husband believed that I still needed guidance with physical therapy. Thus, about six weeks after I completed outpatient therapy, he hired Samantha. She had been the physical therapist who had worked with me in Scenic View when I was still in 4A. Samantha lived a short distance away and she came to my house once each week.

Samantha gave me practical ideas on how to improve my function in my house. She showed me how to take my cane up and down the stairs and how to go to the bathroom at night using my cane instead of sidestepping with the bars on my wall.

More Adjustments

Samantha also practiced walking with me outside on my driveway. Walking on an unlevel surface was difficult at first, because I had to keep shifting my center of balance. I had not realized that when walking uphill a person automatically leans forward and when walking downhill one automatically leans backwards. Samantha pointed this out to me. It seemed simple enough, but my brain had to learn this concept all over again. Since my driveway is not level, it was the perfect place to practice and improve.

I had purchased ankle and wrist weights to wear around my left ankle shortly after I had come home from the hospital. The ankle weight helped me walk better, since it weighed down on my foot and made it easier to place it correctly on the ground. I also started wearing the weights on my wrists when I did arm exercises and used the arm pedal. Though it was more taxing, I thought it was more effective for my recovery.

By this time, I used my quad cane to go from room to room in my house and no longer relied on my wheelchair. Nonetheless, I continued using the wheelchair as a chair at the table, since I was unable to slide myself under the table with a regular chair. Samantha encouraged me to stop using the wheelchair in the house altogether. I brought a dining room armchair into the kitchen, and I was able to slide it in and out at the table. I put the cushion from the wheelchair on it for additional height. Since my dining room is carpeted, using the chair there proved to be a problem; it would not slide on the floor. As always, my husband found a solution and purchased an office chair with wheels for me to use in the dining room.

During the early summer months, Shloimy began taking his first hesitant steps. I watched in amazement as he began walking around while pushing a toy on wheels or even a cardboard box. Eventually, he began taking steps independently. Each time he fell, he just picked himself up and tried again.

I knew that learning to walk could never be as simple for me. If I were to fall, I would risk breaking some bones and being unable to get back up. As I watched him, I secretly hoped I would be able to walk by the time he did. I knew I was being unrealistic, but I could not help feeling a sense of competition.

Libby had turned two at the end of June. She had become very bored during the day and constantly bothered Shloimy. I knew it would be best for everyone to let her have some structured social time outside of the house. I did some research and found a nice playgroup that offered transportation. Though it was hard for me to begin sending her out, I knew it was the right thing to do.

I wanted Libby to adjust to the school setting before putting her on the playgroup van, so on the first day, Zeldy took her and accompanied her to class. I was saddened about it, but it was not feasible for me to go. In the afternoon, though, I was able to wait for her in the minivan while Zeldy went in to pick her up from class. Libby smiled broadly as she came into the van, and she continued going happily every day. As expected, the days at home became much easier, and both Libby and Shloimy were much happier.

In September, another brother of mine became engaged. Since the *kallah* was from Monsey, the *vort* was local. The

More Adjustments

vort was planned in a wheelchair accessible hall so that I would be able to attend. Thankfully, I had a much better experience this time. The hall was large and spacious, and I felt more comfortable. Some ladies sat down to talk to me and speaking was not as difficult as before. We stayed for a little less than an hour, and I enjoyed every minute of it!

Several days later, on September 11, my other brother got married. My makeup was done by a professional makeup artist who came to my house and also helped me with my *shaitel*. Though I was still seeing double, I did not wear my eye patch, so as not to attract unwanted attention. Kasia accompanied me to the wedding to assist me when needed. I also brought Libby and left Shloimy at home with Zeldy and Yitzchok.

I had been looking forward to this *simchah* and to seeing family members I had not seen in awhile. Things started on the wrong foot, however, as the hall had no handicap accessible bathroom. Kasia struggled to help me in the tiny stalls. After that hurdle was behind us, I had a wonderful time. I felt like a celebrity, as everyone came over to greet me and wish me well.

During the dancing, I became disheartened as I watched the lively circle. I was quite envious and wished I could join. I went home feeling somewhat disappointed; I had thought I would feel more normal at such an event by now. Besides, I could not help fretting about the future and worrying whether I would ever be able to dance again.

My friend Tzipporah remembers:

Well, what can I say, Rivkah? I've known you for 14 years now! You have always been an exceptional individual. Despite many challenges, you persevered and worked hard to make your circumstances improve. If you couldn't make them physically improve, you improved them in your mind. That's why I was shocked after visiting you in Scenic View. I had spoken to you initially while you were in Phoenix and your speech was slurred and unclear. I was horrified. I asked you if you knew about this possible outcome in advance and your response was, "No, but I'm lucky to be alive." I then asked if they made a mistake and you said, "No, but brain surgery is always a great risk." There you were, again putting everything in a positive light.

When I visited you in Scenic View, you kept crying and again I was horrified. You were not at all the Rivkah I knew. The Rivkah I knew always saw the cup as half full, even if everyone else on the planet saw it as empty. The Rivkah I knew always had a nice word to say and was always making others feel good, no matter what. We now know your behavior was affected by the steroids, but at the time, I was devastated. My little daughter came with me and afterwards she always talked about

More Adjustments

Mommy's friend with the broken leg (the brace) and one eye (the patch).

Our Rivkah was really there after all, but I only saw the steroids. I came out thinking, "Who knows how long it will be, if ever, until Rivkah will be back?" I went from visiting you directly to a family chasunah. I was so shaken up from the experience that everyone at the chasunah heard about you and your plight. I spoke to you on the phone numerous times, but since I lived in Michigan at the time, I didn't see you again until I moved back to New Jersey.

One of the first things I did (literally!) after I moved was visit you. I had to see how you were doing. At that time, you had organized game playing for therapy, so I took a slot. You beat me hands down and then I knew everything would be okay. You also tried to make me feel better about losing, telling me that you played these games all the time and I probably didn't have time for them. I still remember that we played Blokus Trigon. You were so matter of fact about your situation, so positive and upbeat. I was relieved it had been the steroids after all.

This past summer, I went through my own mini-challenge, and I drew upon many of the things I learnt from you to manage my own situation. I learned how to be a taker when necessary and to make people feel good (I'm still working on that one...). I learned that nothing would happen to my children if they have to go away until I am better, as long as I maintain the proper perspective and don't lose myself. I also learned that I am able to make scary situations seem less frightening, if I phrase them correctly.

Rivkah, you are one amazing person, from whom I am constantly learning. I am amazed by your courage and strength. You give me such chizuk every time I speak to you!

Tzipporah

12
Yomim Tovim

Rosh Hashanah and Sukkos were approaching. We had to start preparing for the *yomim tovim*, especially since Zeldy was expecting a baby on Sukkos. We could not leave anything for the last minute.

A few weeks before Rosh Hashanah, I sat down with Zeldy and wrote a list of all the different dishes we would need for *yom tov*. Afterwards, I wrote a list of all the necessary ingredients and included them with my grocery order. During the following two or three weeks, Zeldy cooked and froze everything for *yom tov*. By cooking twice as much food as we needed each night and freezing half, she also prepared many suppers for after she would give birth. In addition, Zeldy cleaned and seasoned raw chickens and froze them in trays, which were ready to just pop into the oven. Zeldy clearly labeled each dish as she placed it in the freezer.

As Zeldy approached her due date, I asked Kasia to take on more responsibilities. She began doing tasks that Zeldy had been doing, such as taking care of the laundry and bathing my children. Libby was not happy with this change in her bedtime routine, but the problem was easily solved with some bathtub crayons.

Meanwhile, there were more adjustments on the horizon. Kasia planned to return to Poland right after Sukkos, and Zeldy and Yitzchok hoped to move into their own place after their baby was born. I would have to find a replacement for Kasia to assist me and keep the house clean and a replacement for Zeldy to cook and care for the children.

Though I did not know how I would find two suitable people on such short notice, I tried to put my worries aside during *yom tov*. I focused on the present, enjoying each *yom tov* spent with my family. For Rosh Hashanah, Zeldy even managed to prepare fresh food, so that the meals in the freezer would last longer. On Yom Kippur, Kasia came and cared for the children, so that Zeldy and I could fast and *daven* uninterrupted.

Before Sukkos, I decided to hire additional help for *yom tov*. With Zeldy due any day, I could not risk being left alone without her. I placed an ad in the local Jewish classifieds, and it was answered by Miriam, a seventeen-year-old girl who was boarding locally. Miriam stayed with us for the entire Sukkos and helped with the children, setting and clearing the table and serving the *seudos*. It was indeed fortunate that we had hired her, since Zeldy gave birth to a baby girl on the first day of *chol hamoed*.

Yomim Tovim

After resting for one week at a mother and baby convalescent home, Zeldy returned to our house. She spent most of her time upstairs, and I gradually grew accustomed to managing without her constant presence. I hoped that with this arrangement it would not be so hard for me when they were ready to move out.

Since Zeldy was busy with her baby, Kasia took care of Shloimy during the day and was not available to take me to the mall for my walking practice anymore. I arranged with a cousin, my sister in-law and a friend to help. With their assistance, I was able to continue exercising each day. At this point, I felt confident enough to walk without the gait belt, so anyone was able to walk with me.

We were nearing the date of Kasia's departure and I still had no idea what we would do once she left. The Ehrmann family, who had hosted my children over Pesach, had a twenty-year-old daughter named Raizel. Raizel had just completed a computer course but had not yet found a job. She offered to stay with us to care for the children and prepare meals until we found someone permanent.

I was secure and comfortable with Raizel, since she is one of the oldest of a large family and experienced in helping run a busy household. She is also outgoing and *geshikt* and has a wonderful sense of humor. I enjoyed her company, too, and was happy to have her stay with us.

In addition to her wonderful personality, Raizel was also a perfect candidate to take over Zeldy's duties temporarily since she had already spent some Shabbosos in my home and was familiar with our routine. I had been inviting girls every Shabbos for some time, to keep me company and play games with me during the long Shabbos afternoons. After Zeldy had her baby, I also needed someone to help care for the children and serve the *seudos*. Usually two friends came together and among our regulars were Raizel and her sister. Indeed, I was fortunate to have these wonderful, helpful girls each week.

Shortly after Sukkos, on October 31, my next brother got married in the same hall as my other brother. This time I knew to anticipate the problems using the narrow bathroom stall, and since Kasia had already returned to Poland, I had to rely on my husband for assistance. We also took along a teenage girl to help us out, since we brought Libby again. As before, the dancing awakened a deep longing within me. Since my expectations were more realistic now and I had gotten six more weeks of recovery, I was able to enjoy this wedding more than the previous one.

By now, Zeldy and Yitzchok had found an apartment, which was available for them on November 1. I wanted to express my deep appreciation to this selfless, caring couple, but I knew that nothing could sufficiently repay them for all they had done. In the end, I wrote the following poem for Zeldy. I typed it and asked someone to frame it for me. We were both overcome by emotion when I presented it to her. I felt it was the best way for me to say thank you.

Dear Zeldy,

Well how should I say this?
It's hard to express.
It's not that easy,

I must confess.
I have to thank you,
In the appropriate way,
But I don't know
where to start,

Yomim Tovim

There is so much to say.
You've been mother to my kids,
For quite a long while.
While I was away,
In my own exile.
You bathed them,
And dressed them,
And gave them to eat.
Kissed booboos away,
No easy feat.
You did all the cooking,
And laundry and more.
You were kept very busy,
Of that I am sure.
You got up at night,
When Shloimy wouldn't sleep.
Without a complaint,
Not even a peep.
What should I say?
You did it with grace.
As if the kids were your own,
With a smile on your face.
You washed their hands each morning.
And said shema each night.
You showed them good middos,
And love for yiddishkeit.
I feel very indebted,
More than I can say.
You did so much for me,
That I cannot repay.
Hashem will have to,
Repay what I owe,
Brocha and hatzlochah,
Through your home will flow.
You will have nachas from your children
And a life of success.
Full of good things,
With joy and happiness.

With loads of love,
Rivkah

The Zeldy and Yitzchok era was now over, as they moved out as scheduled. The house seemed quite empty without them. There was more space, since their furniture had been moved out, but their absence was sorely felt.

As I looked back at the previous four months, I marveled at how two couples, who had not known each other previously, had managed to live together for almost half a year without having a single disagreement. This was testimony to the outstanding *middos* of both Zeldy and Yitzchok, who were easygoing and sensitive people. They had cared for my children with true devotion, yet Zeldy had not been afraid to be strict with or discipline Libby in front of me when necessary. I had not always had the energy to negotiate and was glad when Zeldy took over. Now, after they moved out, I was forced to fall back into the role of mother and take charge of my home again.

Kasia had departed shortly before they moved out, and we hired a woman named Lilly to assist me in the morning. Lilly was a nursing student who worked the night shift at a group home for girls nearby. She came each morning for one hour on her way home from work to help me shower and dress and to prepare my breakfast. Lilly also came on Shabbos mornings, which was helpful to my husband, who usually assisted me throughout Shabbos.

While things were working out even better than expected with Raizel and Lilly, we knew that they were both filling their positions only temporarily. The search was still on for someone who was available to replace Kasia on a long-term basis.

Luckily, the wife of my husband's Polish business associate offered to put an ad in the Polish newspaper for us. She screened all the callers who responded and gave my husband the names and phone numbers of those who seemed most suitable.

After reviewing the information, my husband called down one woman for an interview. Dorothy was slim and of average height with curly dark hair that bounced around her shoulders. She did not speak English well and brought along her sister in-law to act as an interpreter.

My husband is a good judge of people and can usually pick up on their character right away. He was immediately impressed and ready to hire her. Though I was worried about the language barrier, I decided to trust his decision.

Raizel remained for a couple of weeks to train Dorothy, who had moved into the extra bedroom. Dorothy was intelligent and learned everything quickly, and within two weeks, we were able to communicate. My children took to her immediately, and she was pleasant to have around. Dorothy was organized and meticulous; she cleaned up and organized my pantry, laundry room, linen closet and coat closet. She washed the walls and the windows inside and out and even cleaned up outside in the backyard. It felt wonderful to have a clean and organized home.

Around this time, I had my *shaitel* washed and set and started wearing it every day. It felt great to look at my reflection in the mirror and see how much better I looked. I also wanted to start wearing makeup for Shabbos, but since my right hand was still impaired, I asked Raizel to help me get ready each *erev* Shabbos. With her assistance, I was able to greet Shabbos wearing make-up, my *shaitel* and Shabbos earrings.

One Friday, when Raizel helped me get ready for Shabbos, she could not find my earrings. I kept them in a little red box with my other earrings on my dresser, but the box had disappeared. On a whim, I asked her to see if she could find my gold and diamond necklace, which I also kept on the dresser. Raizel could not locate it either, and I realized that my jewelry had probably been stolen.

My husband told me to ask Lilly to put my Shabbos earrings on me the next morning and watch her reaction. I did as he advised and Lilly could not find my earrings either. She rummaged through the dresser and suddenly found the box; it was suspiciously rolled up inside one of my snoods. I then asked her to make sure my necklace was also there. I hoped she would find it the same way, but she did not.

"I think I'll organize my dresser with you tomorrow," I told her. "It's too cluttered and I cannot find anything." I hoped that if she had indeed taken the necklace, she would bring it back and save face by 'finding' it when we cleaned up together.

The next day, Sunday, Lilly helped me organize my dresser, but my necklace did not turn up. As a result, my husband decided to let her go. "We can't have two workers in the house," he told me, "because if something disappears we don't know who took it."

Thus, he told Lilly that he could not afford to keep two aides and that Dorothy would help me each morning from then on. (I found the necklace two years later, when I was able to go through my things myself. It had been put away with the rest of my jewelery. I don't know who put it there because it wasn't me or my husband)

I worried whether Dorothy would be able to manage taking care of both me and the children in the morning. I decided to get up a half hour earlier than usual, so that she would have time to help me get ready before tending to the kids.

Yomim Tovim

While she helped them get ready, I returned to bed for my leg exercises, and afterwards we all went down together for breakfast. This new routine worked well, and I was pleased with the change.

During the first two weeks, Raizel taught Dorothy how to cook all my recipes and prepare for Shabbos. She taught her how to keep *milchig* and *fleishig* separate, set the table for Shabbos and wash the children *negel vasser* in the morning. Dorothy was a conscientious student and learned everything quickly. I saw my husband was correct in his judgment, and I had no reason to worry.

With Zeldy not running my kitchen any longer, it was up to me to direct the cooking. I planned all the menus and prepared shopping lists. When it was time to cook, I checked the eggs and turned on the stove for Dorothy. In the beginning, when she prepared a dish for the first time, I sat in the kitchen and guided her step by step. Before long, she was a real pro and this was no longer necessary.

The *cholent* turned out to be the most challenging dish to prepare, since I'd never followed a recipe and could not provide exact measurements. For several weeks, we wrote down how much we added of each ingredient. We adjusted the recipe each time until it was finally perfect. Since then, I have never had a guest who did not like my *cholent*, so I'm sharing my recipe here. (I don't include beans, because I do not like them, but they can be added if desired.)

My cholent recipe:

4 medium red potatoes, cubed
2 carrots, chopped
1 c. barley
2 marrow bones
2-3 strips flanken
3-4 tsp. paprika
2 Tbsp. honey
4 tsp. salt
1/4 tsp. cayenne pepper
1 tsp. garlic powder
1 large onion, chopped
5 c. water

We put all ingredients in a crock-pot and set the temperature on high. Shortly before Shabbos, we mixed everything and turned down the temperature to "keep warm." By Shabbos morning, it was perfect.

There were several other recipes that we wrote down and recorded after some trial and error. Eventually, the dishes started coming out the same each time and my husband appreciated the consistency.

Since we were focusing on perfecting my recipes, I decided to improve my handwriting by reorganizing my collection of recipes. I had all my recipes on index cards in a box, and I purchased a recipe book and rewrote them all neatly there.

I started feeling happier and more content as my hard work began paying off and I saw constant improvement.

In addition, I felt accomplished as I helped keep my home running smoothly through delegating how and what should be done. Of course, I still had my fair share of frustrations, but it felt good to be productive again.

Despite all the progress, I was still exasperated by my constant dependence on others. I could not get myself a snack or drink, answer the telephone if it was not beside me, pick up things that fell to the floor, or simply turn the lights on or off. I felt like a small child who had to ask for everything.

Libby was smart enough to recognize my limitations, and she often took advantage of my handicaps. Once, when she was upstairs with me, she began scribbling on the wall with a black permanent marker. I told her to stop, but she just kept going, knowing I could not get up to take it away from her. Another time, I was in the kitchen with the children while Dorothy was upstairs. Libby held a baby bottle upside down, dripping its contents onto Shloimy's head. I repeatedly told her to stop, but she just ignored me. In desperation, I finally threw a plastic cup at her. It did not hurt her, but it frightened her enough to make her stop. Similarly, when she ran away with the Chinese checkers' marbles or finger painted the wall with diaper rash cream, I could not stop her. It was distressing not to be able to discipline my own child.

With Shloimy, I also often felt powerless in my inability to parent him properly. When he teethed at night, for instance, I awoke from his screams. I knew that Dorothy was taking care of him, but it was so hard to hear him cry and to be unable to help him myself. This inability to care for my children was one of the hardest parts of my entire ordeal.

Though parenting provided challenges, my children often made me smile as they tried to be my little helpers. Whenever I wanted to use the bathroom, for example, Libby ran ahead to open the door for me. Sometimes she even climbed up and turned on the light or closed the door behind me once I was inside. She realized on her own that these little things were hard for me and wanted to help.

Similarly, whenever I was doing exercise with the clothes pins, some inevitably fell to the floor. Shloimy loved to pick them up for me. He also liked bringing me items I needed, such as the telephone or my quad cane. The cane was quite heavy for him, and he carried it with both hands when I asked for it.

At the time, I was still wearing my eye patch. Every six weeks I bought a new supply, and each time I hoped it would be the last time I purchased them. I still had double vision, and though I had tried to go without a patch on several occasions, I was still too uncomfortable. I knew I would have to wait it out and continued doing my exercise with the laser pointer in bed each night.

During the winter months, things settled into a calm routine. Libby went happily to playgroup with the van every day. Shloimy stayed home and began bonding with me and calling me Mommy. Dorothy managed the house proficiently, and I didn't have to supervise her much. I also kept busy on my computer and by playing games with visitors twice each day. Dorothy went home each Friday afternoon and returned on Sunday morning. During Shabbos, I continued having high school girls stay with us to help set the table, serve and care for the children.

Granted, things were not exactly the way I would have liked them to be, but I was grateful knowing that my home was running as smoothly as possible under the circumstances.

13
Winter 2006-2007

*I*n December of 2006, I started pushing a shopping cart in the grocery, instead of sitting in the wheelchair. I put Shloimy inside to give the cart stability, because I lost my balance when it was light and went too quickly. At first, I would go to the store with a list of three items, but after getting only two, I would head to the register feeling too exhausted to continue. I slowly built up my endurance until, by the end of December, I walked about thirty-five minutes with the cart three times each week.

Shortly after my surgery, a friend contacted BINA, an organization that provides guidance and support to individuals affected by stroke or brain injury. From time to time, Chavie, the founder and director of the organization, would call to inquire about my progress and inform me of various therapeutic methods. For a long time, I was too busy to start anything new. In December, Chavie called again and recommended that I begin aqua therapy. This time, I finally felt ready to add a new therapy to my schedule.

Thus, I once again began visiting Scenic View, going once a week for aqua therapy. In the water, a person is about eighty percent lighter than on dry land. It is much easier to move and the force of gravity is not as strong. As a result, I was able to work on my balance, coordination and muscle strength in ways that would be impossible outside of the pool.

During my sessions, I walked forwards, backwards and sideways while holding onto a stabilizer. The stabilizer is a pole with a float at each end, and it helps a person balance while walking in the water. My therapist also guided me through various other exercises, and after only one week, I already noticed an improvement in my balance. By the third session, I was able to walk forward in the water without using a stabilizer.

I soon saw other improvements, too. At first, my therapist had to put a weight around my left ankle to weigh it down and prevent my left foot from curling inward. Otherwise, I was unable to put my foot flat on the floor of the pool. After only a couple of times, my therapist forgot to put on the weight. We realized then that I was able to put my foot down properly. My therapist asked whether I could put my foot flat on the floor out of the water without my brace, and I did not know the answer. That night at home, as I made my way from my bed to the bathroom without the brace, I realized that my left foot and ankle had significantly improved since I had begun aqua therapy.

Winter 2006-2007

Seeing how beneficial the water therapy was, I soon started going twice weekly for forty-five minutes each time. Dorothy accompanied me in the water, and Zehava Pearl watched Shloimy when we went.

Sometimes, while I was at Scenic View, I visited some of the nurses who had taken care of me when I was there as an inpatient. They were always happy to see me. They had seen me when I was at my worst, and it was nice for them to see me recovering.

One day, I wrote a thank you poem to Angel, the nurse's aide who had been my primary caregiver on 4A. I typed it, printed it out and asked Dorothy to frame it and wrap it for me. When I visited Scenic View for aqua therapy, I went up to present it to her. Needless to say, Angel was genuinely touched.

Dear Angel,

It's been more than
   six months,
I feel it is time.
I would like to say thanks,
In the form of a rhyme.
My stay in rehab,
Was hard and long.
I cried a lot,
Everything was wrong.
I was numb, had
   double vision,
And couldn't move
   my left side.

I felt like I was spinning,
On a roller coaster ride.
But there was one light,
That helped me through.
I wouldn't have survived,
If not for you.
You took me to the bathroom,
When I needed to go.
And got me dressed
   in the morning,
So I looked just so.
You did everything with
   a gracious smile,
And made me laugh,

STRUGGLE TO THE SUMMIT

In times of trial.
As hard as it was,
And I wanted it to end.
At least I felt like,
I had a good friend.
Again I want to say thanks,

For all the kindness and care.
I'll be forever grateful,
To the nurse of the year.
Fondly,

Rivkah Zucker

At the end of that year, I hosted a Chanukah gathering for my family once again in my home. It was nice to see everyone and hard to believe that it had been only one year ago, during the previous Chanukah gathering in December of 2005, when I had mentioned to some family members that I was experiencing some unusual symptoms. It seemed like a lifetime had passed since then!

Around that time, my husband's brother became engaged. The *vort* was in Brooklyn, but this time I decided not to go. I did not mind traveling, but I disliked being parked in a corner at such events, watching the crowd from the sidelines. I usually enjoy social gatherings and parties, but in the state I was in, such functions only distressed me. Sometimes acquaintances asked why I did not attend one event or another, and it was frustrating for me when I explained my feelings but continued to feel misunderstood.

My days were full, as I kept exercising and practicing new skills to accelerate the recovery process. I began playing computer games every day to help improve my hand-eye coordination. At first, I could barely pass the first levels of the game, but with time I improved tremendously. I also still played games with visitors for one hour on mornings that I did not go to Scenic View and for another hour from eight to nine o'clock in the evenings. In addition, Samantha, my physical therapist, continued coming once each week.

One morning in early December, I was sitting at the kitchen table, while Dorothy was bustling around doing housework. Libby was at playgroup, and Shloimy was happily playing at home. I sat there thinking about how everyone was going about their daily lives, while I was stuck in a wheelchair with only a pen and notebook within reach. I felt useless and helpless and decided to write a letter to Hashem. I started with "Dear Hashem," and after that, the words just flowed. I cried as I wrote each word. It was still difficult for me to *daven*, but this felt like a real *tefillah*, coming from the depths of my heart.

At first, I kept my letter private, but then I realized that it contained a powerful message and had to be shared with other people. Indeed, this is the poem that appears at the beginning of this book and has previously been published in the Binah Magazine.

After composing and publishing the letter, I decided that I wanted to share my story. I made up my mind to write a book and started a journal of my recovery. As I wrote all the details of my experience up until that point, I discovered that there was a therapeutic value to recording all the traumatic events of the past year. As I wrote about each incident, I transferred all the pain and distress to the computer. I felt that I was being cleansed of these unpleasant memories and no longer replayed them in my mind afterwards. Here is one of my early entries:

STRUGGLE TO THE SUMMIT

December 28, 2006

>This might sound silly, but I feel this is a big accomplishment. Yesterday I reached the end of the computer game I play for my coordination. Before my surgery, it was easy for me to get to the end. It takes speed, control and good hand-eye coordination. I am on the way back to my old self!

In addition to writing in my journal, I also started writing and framing thank you poems for people who had helped me get through the past twelve months. I felt that this was the only way to express my appreciation. Following is the poem I wrote to Zehava Pearl, who had been there every step of the way, helping and supporting me in whatever way necessary.

Dear Zehava,
Now is the time
For a poem just for you,
To say words of thanks,
For all that you do.
During my hospital stay,
You did laundry and shopping,
I counted on you,
I kept you quite hopping.
You planned a rotation
Of who should come when,
'Cause I was so lonely
And needed it then.
You got me my health food,
Sent a protein drink,
And took care of my needs,
When I couldn't think.
And for Pesach you cooked,
All the food, every dish,
We had a whole spread
Chicken, kugels and fish.
When I finally came home,
You didn't stop there,
You arranged different help,
And continued your care.
You're on call all the time,
Offering help and advice,
You give of yourself,
Without thinking twice.

Winter 2006-2007

Each morning and night,
Two times every day,
You arrange for some women,
To come and to play.
The list is quite endless,
I can just keep on going,
My hakaros hatov to you,
Keeps on flowing.
There are no adequate words,
To thank you enough,
Thanks will have to do,
Cause I'm finding it tough.
But there is more than just thanks
That I need to say,
Brachos and simchos,
Should come your way.
Hashem will reward you,
For your chessed and aid,
And He will take care,
And make sure you're well paid.

With Love and appreciation,
Rivkah

At the end of December, Samantha began focusing on exercises to strengthen my left leg. My left leg was still not strong enough to support me, and I could not lift my right leg off the floor for even a second without support. In order for me to eventually get rid of the cane, my left leg had to become much stronger. To strengthen it, I started standing at the kitchen sink and lifting my right foot off the floor putting my full body weight onto my left leg and using my arms and the counter for support. I tried to do this for a few minutes at a time twice a day.

As I continued looking for exercises that would help increase my independence, I noted five specific areas which required improvement: I had to regain my balance, my strength and my coordination and rid myself of the numbness and double vision. Somehow, when I broke it down into smaller, individual issues, it did not seem as difficult to conquer.

January 5, 2007

> *I can't wait to be able to move and balance normally. When I am out shopping at the supermarket, I observe how people stand and move. There are people who stand on only one foot and put the other one up on the shopping cart when they wait on line. People just saunter around pushing the cart with one hand and talking on their cell phone with their other one. I need both hands to keep my balance, and I have to stand with both feet on the ground at the same time when I wait in line.*

I also observed how easily people slipped in and out of their cars. I had to sit down on the seat with both of my feet still on the ground and then swivel into the car. I could not even recall how this feat was usually accomplished. I watched closely as other people opened the car door and put their first leg into the car while standing on their other leg. I longed to be able to this again.

While my movement was still limited, there was much to hope for. I was feeling energetic again and sleeping well at night. I was in good overall health and had an encouraging prognosis for a complete recovery. I was optimistic and motivated and aspired to be fully functional and back to myself. Moreover, I was prepared to put in a great deal of effort to get there.

One day, Chavie from BINA contacted me again and recommended that I look into the Feldenkrais method, a method of reeducating the brain on how to use the muscles most effectively by using correct patterns of movement. I followed her advice and began visiting Dr. Robbie Ofir, a practitioner of the Feldenkrais method who lives in Manhattan. I saw Robbie each Sunday for an hour and a half and gained tremendously from these sessions.

Robbie saw people in his own home, an apartment in a high-rise building. He had a large table that was quite low and covered with a slippery vinyl. He instructed me to lie on my left side and make my head comfortable on a pillow. Once I was in the correct position, Robbie guided me in various movements and gave me awareness of the muscles that worked together. For example, he told me to press my lower knee downward into the table and asked if I felt any other part of my body move at the same time. I noticed that my pelvis would rotate a little when I did this. Thus, Robbie showed me how the whole body is connected and how one movement is directly related to another.

Robbie went through a whole series of small movements with me, explaining that these are designed to help re-pattern the brain. "By coordinating your movements while lying down without the force of gravity hindering you," he explained, "you can perfect the patterns of movement and your walking will become more coordinated and smooth."

Robbie also told me that it is important to work on the quality, not the quantity, of my gait. "If more walking would improve the quality of a person's walk," he said, "then mail carriers, who walk around all day, would be the best walkers.

True, you have to work on your endurance to be able to walk longer, but once the quality of your walk improves, you will automatically be able to walk for greater distances."

Before I left, Robbie advised me to relive our session at home and do the exercises he showed me. "The exercises should be easy to do, not strenuous," he reminded me.

I started doing them each morning and night in bed. Though I did not feel that I was accomplishing much, I followed the exercise regimen religiously. Surprisingly, after only a couple of weeks of sessions and home exercises, I noticed subtle differences in my movements and felt my walking become smoother and more coordinated.

January 16, 2007

> The other night Shloimy woke up at around five o'clock in the morning. I heard him crying, but Dorothy did not. It is such a helpless feeling to hear my baby crying and not be able to do anything about it. I called Dorothy on her cell phone, and she went to Shloimy. He was teething and wouldn't calm down. My husband took him into his bed, but he still cried. Tylenol didn't settle him either.
>
> It is not easy to take him into my bed. I still cannot move around well, and I can't move him either. Since nothing was working, I asked my husband to put him on my stomach with his head resting on me. That worked for a few minutes, but then he started crying again. I asked my husband

to move him comfortably resting on my arm. That calmed him down. After a few minutes, I was no longer comfortable, so I asked Shloimy if he wants to go to Tatty. He said "No." Then I asked him if he wants to stay in Mommy's bed and he said "Yeah." I ended up waiting about half an hour until he fell asleep and then my husband moved him to his bed.

It was such a warm feeling having my baby fall asleep in my bed. Even though I wasn't comfortable, I was happy to have him sleep next to me. I was also pleased that he preferred me over my husband. It showed me that we are bonding well and he is becoming attached to me.

Last night Libby wanted to come out of her crib after Dorothy put her in for the night. She was crying, and Dorothy couldn't quiet her down. I decided to go upstairs to her room and sing her some songs. I still can't sing properly. I don't have the strength in my voice yet, but Libby likes my singing. I went upstairs and walked to her crib. I stood holding onto the crib and sang her a few songs. She then went to sleep happily and calmly. It was uplifting to be doing something a normal mother does. It wasn't easy, and I don't plan to do it every night, but when it's necessary, I know I am able.

Though these incidents may seem insignificant, they meant the world to me. I was unable to do any childcare at all, but here and there, I tried. I felt wonderful when I could act as a mother to my children.

January 20, 2007

This morning I took both of my children out of their cribs by myself. I walked into their rooms, lowered the crib bar and took them out with my right hand. I used the crib and my left hand to keep my balance. They helped by holding onto my arm, and I was able to lower them onto the floor. I still cannot carry them for even one step.

The other day Shloimy was sitting on my lap when I was using the computer. He pulled out the rubber of his ponytail, which is like a fountain on top of his head. He was in a good position for me to put it back in. Though it was challenging, I did manage to make a new ponytail for him.

This morning I put on both of my children's shoes. They each brought me their shoes, and I lifted them up on the table in front of me with their feet on my lap. Shloimy' shoes close with Velcro and Libby's are tie shoes, and I managed to close both.

One day I asked Samantha how long she thought I would still need to walk with a cane.

"I can't predict," she replied, "but I think you will still need assistance in your walking with some sort of device for about another year."

While I was still in Scenic View, I had had a similar conversation with her about the wheelchair. Back then, I had fallen apart at the news that I would definitely go home with a wheelchair. I had viewed everything in black and white and was unable to visualize a midway between being completely helpless and fully recovered. Now, I understood that I would improve progressively, but it would not happen overnight. Thus, while my situation would not be exactly the same in a year, I would still need assistance as I continued working towards a complete recovery.

My therapist Samantha remembers:

Rivkah, I met you shortly after your arrival at the acute inpatient rehab. This was the start of our relationship, which would slowly unfold over the course of many months. Interestingly enough, however, my first impression of you was quite similar to how I would describe you today. That's because the most impressive thing about you is not your physical condition, superficial appearance or whether you're seated in a chair or standing on your own two feet. The most noticeable quality lies within your heart and mind. This is your determination, unrelenting in your drive to succeed. I was always impressed by your level of inner strength and confidence. I believe this positive attitude truly carried you throughout your recovery. Rivkah, you are blessed with many gifts and are truly an example of how motivation delivers success. I am very proud of you and your accomplishments thus far and eager to see you continue this journey.

14
One Year Post-Op

Towards the end of January, Dorothy dropped a bombshell on us. Her seven-year-old daughter, who was back in Poland, was not doing well in her absence, and she had decided to go home. She had already booked a ticket and would be leaving in two weeks time.

Obviously, I was quite distressed at the news. Of course, I understood her desire to return home quickly, but we had been pleased with Dorothy, and I worried about finding a replacement. I was also anxious to find someone quickly so that Dorothy would still be able to train her. The person's responsibilities would include childcare, housekeeping and cooking; she had to be able to drive and be willing to assist me in the pool during aqua therapy. I also needed assistance while I showered and dressed each morning. Additionally she had to be intelligent and have a pleasant personality. It was a hard bill to fill.

Before looking for someone new, we decided to contact Kasia. Prior to her return to Poland she had told me that she planned to come back in February.

To our relief, Kasia informed us that she was indeed returning on February 10 and would be happy to work for us again. She was not sure how long she would stay, but she was willing to work from seven thirty in the morning until eight o'clock in the evening. I was so thankful that everything would work out well.

Dorothy's last week with us was complicated and challenging in several ways. First, she came down with the flu and could not work properly. When she finally felt a little better, she felt bad about her time in bed and overexerted herself much too quickly. This caused her to relapse and become even weaker. I had some help from a few girls, and we tried our best to manage.

On Wednesday evening, just as things were settling down, my husband tripped outside and severely hurt his ankle. He went to the emergency room, where the doctor established that it was sprained. He was given crutches to get around and told to keep off his foot. He came home after both Dorothy and I were in bed and had to serve himself supper despite his condition. When he came up to the bedroom, I wondered aloud what would happen if Shloimy woke up. We were three handicapped adults taking care of two toddlers. The situation would have been comical if we had not felt so desperate.

Of course, Shloimy woke up crying at eleven thirty. My husband managed to hobble into his room and bring him back to his bed, where he slept for the rest of the night.

One Year Post-Op

Thursday morning Dorothy miraculously felt better. Though not completely recovered, she was well enough to begin doing some tasks around the house. My husband, on the other hand, could not get around and had to stay home from work. During his brief experience of immobility, he told me that he was able to appreciate what I was going through a little bit more.

Dorothy's last day with us was Friday. My husband asked me to write a poem for her, since she had truly been incredibly devoted. I had not planned to write one since her English was not that good. Nonetheless, my husband thought she would appreciate it, so I took his advice.

Dear Dorothy,

It's time for you to leave
Homeward on your way,
I understand your
 need to go,
But I wish that you
 could stay.
You've been a real asset
 to my home,
And kept it running well,
Anyone walking
 through my door,
It was easy for them to tell.
It was obvious to all,
That you did your
 job just right,
That you cleaned up
 everything,
Before retiring for the night.
All the laundry and
 the dishes,
You kept very up to date,
Washing everything
 right away,
I never had to wait.
My pantry, linen closet,
Laundry room and
 kitchen drawer,
You organized real well,
Even better than before.
The food here's not
 like home,
But you learned to
 make each dish,
From the schnitzel
 to the cholent,

STRUGGLE TO THE SUMMIT

Even gefilte fish.
The fantastic care you
   gave my kids,
Was just the best, it
   was top rate.
You took care of them for me,
Cause I couldn't in my state.
Shloimy learned to
   say your name,
In his own special way.
Dorty, Dorty, Dorty,
The whole day, was
   what he'd say.
You drove me to Manhattan,
Every Sunday without fail,
You took out all the garbage,
And brought me all my mail.
Not only did you take me to,
My water therapy,
You even got yourself all wet,
In the pool with me.
You also took me shopping,
And helped me
   guide the cart,
We went together
   all the time,
To stores such as Wal-Mart.
When you first came
   you didn't know,
English very well,

But you were quick in
   how you learned,
And now you're
   talking swell.
Although tablespoon
   and teaspoon,
Had you all confused,
The words have and half
   seemed the same to you,
And had you quite amused.
Now it's time for you to go,
Home across the sea,
Back to your life in Poland,
And to your family.
But before you leave
   and say goodbye,
And wish us all farewell,
There's one more thing
   I need to say,
There's one more
   thing to tell.
Thanks a lot is what it is.
Thanks in every way,
I hope it all works
   out for you,
And good luck I say.

               With great appreciation,
                        Rivkah Zucker

One Year Post-Op

I typed it and bought a nice picture frame. One of the people who came to play games with me put the poem in the frame. Even though Dorothy did not understand every word, she understood the gist of the poem and was truly touched.

Dorothy left on Friday, but there was still a full week until Kasia was scheduled to arrive. During the first couple of days, Raizel and Ruchy Ehrmann took turns coming to our house to help. On Tuesday, a girl from Brooklyn arrived to stay until the end of the week. When Libby returned home from playgroup, she was met by an unfamiliar girl and became hysterical. She cried and cried, refusing to calm down or allow the girl to bathe her or change her at night. In the end, Libby fell asleep crying on the floor.

I felt terrible for my daughter. She'd grown attached to Zeldy, then Kasia and finally Dorothy. Each one stayed for a while and then walked out of her life. Raizel came and went, but Libby grew to love her as well. A new person was just too much for her to handle.

I decided to call Mrs. Ehrmann and explain the situation to her. Raizel was getting married in only five weeks, and I knew she had much to do still. Nonetheless, I begged her to let Raizel come for the next few days. In the end, Raizel kindly agreed to be at our house every morning to send Libby off and return at three o'clock when she came home. A friend offered to stay with me for the few hours in between. The girl from Brooklyn had to be sent home, but she understood the situation and did not take it personally.

February 10, 2007

> I find this whole situation extremely distressing. I can't bare sitting and watching Libby suffer while

I can do absolutely nothing about it. I just want to get up and whip this place back into shape! I wish I could take care of my children, give them their baths, dress them, put them to bed, sit on the floor with them when they play and pick them up to carry them. The ache inside me is so strong, I feel like I'm bursting. I know this is a temporary state, but living through it is so difficult.

I called Libby's teacher today. I want her to understand that Libby is having a hard time at home and to give her a little more attention and TLC. Her teacher told me she noticed that something seems to be troubling her; she has been acting angry and crying easily.

As far as my water therapy is concerned, I haven't gone this week, since there is no one to take me. I haven't gone out to shop and walk with a shopping cart either. The temperature outside has been in the teens all week and the weather kept me indoors. My husband has been helping me get ready each morning, so I haven't done my leg exercises either. I also didn't go to Dr. Ofir in Manhattan this past Sunday, and I won't be going next Sunday. Everything should get back to normal once Kasia comes next week. I hate all this disorder! I know this is just the way it has to be now. Gam zeh y'avar.

We were all relieved when Kasia arrived at last and things finally settled down. Libby seemed pleased, and Shloimy

One Year Post-Op

called her by her name and appeared to remember her from four months earlier.

Several days later, February 14, was the first anniversary of my surgery. I was not even close to where I would have liked to be. My balance was still not too good; I needed a quad cane to walk; and I could only cover short distances at a time. Because of my double vision, I still wore an eye patch. My left side was also still significantly weaker and some numbness remained in my left hand and foot, the left half of my tongue and around my mouth. I had certainly progressed considerably, but there was still a long way to go.

I wrote the following poem on February 18, 2007, expressing my hope for a complete, speedy recovery.

Oh, I can't wait
Until I am able.
To clear off and set,
The Shabbos table.
To cook and prepare
All of the food,
And to properly care for
My little brood.
To just get in the car,
And drive off and go,
Or prepare and knead
The challah dough.
To sit on the floor,
And play with my son,
Or snap some pictures,
Of him having fun.
To vacuum the carpets,
And wash the tiles.
To take a walk,
For a couple of miles.
To go to the store,
And normally shop,
Without getting tired,
And having to stop.
To just be normal,
Capable and able.
To run my home,
Functional and stable.
I am on the mend,
And getting there,

But it's already been
A whole long year.
I'm feeling impatient,
Cause I'm in a hurry.
My progress is slow,
And I'm starting to worry.
But I have to relax,
Cause Hashem will decide,

How long it will take,
And I'm in for the ride.
Hashem knows what's best
And he will make sure
When I'm supposed
to be better,
He will send me a cure.

My first year post-op had come and gone. I had been under the false impression that I would be completely recovered by this time and was quite disappointed. "You misunderstood the doctor," my husband told me. "He said that the fastest recovery is during the first year after surgery, and the recovery process slows down after that, not that it will only take a year to recover."

I had a long conversation with my husband to put things in perspective. We discussed my progress and the probability that it would take at least another year before I was back to myself. Realizing that feeling impatient was counterproductive and would not help me progress any faster, we accepted that my recovery period would probably last a lot longer than we had anticipated. Verbalizing this caused us to feel much better and helped us come to terms with our situation.

During our conversation, I asked my husband, as I had often asked previously, how we were covering the exorbitant fees of my aides and therapies. Though we had always been able to pay our bills, we had never had any significant savings. As always, my husband replied, "Hashem provides."

One Year Post-Op

I never pushed him on the issue, since, frankly, I did not feel up to sharing this burden. I was focusing all my energy on therapy and was immensely relieved that he was handling the financial aspect of the situation.

While I was still in the sub acute unit in Scenic View, the founder and director of BINA visited me. He had suffered a stroke about nine years earlier, when he was still a young man. Subsequently, he and his wife established the BINA organization to provide guidance and support for victims of brain injury and stroke. Though I had not had a stroke, the recovery process was quite similar, and he came to give me *chizuk*. During the visit, he said, "With time, it just gets better and better." Now, whenever I felt frustrated or discouraged, I repeated these words to myself and that made me feel better.

I knew I was doing everything I could to speed up the recovery process. In fact, Robbie was quite impressed when, during one of our sessions, I shared my daily routine and told him about all my therapeutic activities. "There are probably people in a similar situation who just sit and watch TV all day," I speculated, "and they aren't motivated to do so much therapy."

"Yes," he agreed, "there are. They simply exist, but you are living."

Indeed, I did try to live my life as well as possible. In February, I asked my husband to purchase a wireless earpiece for my home phone. My right hand became fatigued after I held the phone for just a few minutes. This little device proved to be life changing for me. I was able to write or walk across the room while I was on the telephone. Even more importantly, I was able to hold a phone conversation comfortably for a normal length of time, instead of the mere five minutes that had been the maximum previously.

Sometime later, I also purchased a three section shampoo/conditioner/body wash dispenser and shower gloves. The dispenser allowed me to get shampoo and body wash with just one hand, and the gloves, which were made out of stretchy, scrubby material, were much easier to wash with, since I did not have to hold anything.

Another item I purchased was a mirror that came with lights and magnification that was designed for applying makeup. Since I still had double vision, this task was quite difficult, but I was determined to start putting on makeup by myself and figured that this would make it much easier.

In this manner, I constantly looked for ways to improve my life and my ability to function as a normal human being. Though the road was never easy, my efforts bore fruit and encouraged me to continue.

Another source of encouragement was remembering where I had been the previous year and how far I had come since then. For example, when Purim arrived at the beginning of March, I thought about the previous Purim when I had spent almost the entire day crying and feeling miserable. Though I had a relatively quiet Purim this year, it was pleasant and enjoyable.

Someone came to my house to read the *megillah* for me both at night and during the day, and we ate the *seudah* with Zehava Pearl's family. Unlike the previous Purim, I was able to open some of the *mishloach manos*. Though few people stopped by, Rabbi Ehrmann spent about an hour at our

One Year Post-Op

house. All the people who went to his home during that time were directed to us, so we had a nice crowd for a while.

The day after Purim, I discovered that I was able to take some steps without using my cane. I was in the bathroom and managed to take four whole steps as I walked from the toilet to the sink. My stronger right leg was able to support me as I moved my left foot forward. Since I had the grab bar right next to me, I felt confident enough to try taking a quick step with my right foot as my left leg supported me. Though the distance I covered was barely three or four feet, it was my own Purim miracle and a source of much encouragement.

Later that day, I told my husband about my achievement. "When I go to the bathroom, I will show you how I do it," I promised proudly.

"If you were able to do it in the bathroom," he replied, "you can do it anywhere else."

The idea excited me, and we decided to try right away. My husband slowly walked backwards in front of me, pulling my walker along as I walked the full loop around my kitchen, hallway and living room. I was overjoyed, feeling that I was one step closer to real walking.

I repeated the exercise each day until my next scheduled visit with Robbie Ofir the following week. During my appointment, I shared my newest milestone with him and enthusiastically told him about my daily walking exercise. "I can walk the entire loop in my house without a cane," I informed him proudly.

"I'm sorry to disappoint you," he said, "but I do not think that you are gaining any therapeutic benefit from that exercise. In fact, it can actually be detrimental for your progress. Walking without a cane will cause you to become good at walking the wrong way. You will develop bad habits in your walking that will be hard to change later."

I had to admit that while I had been practicing walking alone the past few days, it had not been a pretty walk at all. Thus, after hearing his opinion, I resolved to stop doing the exercise.

"What about some of the other things I do to speed up my recovery?" I inquired. "For instance, do you think that wearing weights on my wrists while I do arm exercises is beneficial?"

Robbie asked me to show him the exercises I did with and without the weights. After watching me carefully as I did the exercises, he told me not to use the weights anymore. "When you didn't use the weights," he explained, "you used your right and left sides more evenly. With the weights, you compensated for your weaker left side by leaning over and your posture was compromised."

Robbie taught me the importance of making progress correctly rather than quickly. While focusing on correct movements sometimes seemed to slow me down, in the long run it would help me make greater strides and accelerate my recovery.

Each week, Robbie taught me new exercises that gave me an awareness of my movements. If I was unable to actually move in the way I was supposed to, Robbie told me to imagine it. "If you imagine it first," he told me, "your brain will learn how to move correctly."

One Year Post-Op

By this time, he had taught me close to ten different exercises, engaging muscles in my feet, ankles, legs, knees, pelvis, hips, shoulders, arms, neck and some other joints that I never knew existed. I did all the exercises faithfully, dropping each one only once it became easy. Robbie had explained that once the exercise no longer posed a challenge, I had already benefited from it. Indeed, I saw progress in all areas, and my movements became smoother and more coordinated.

While I was making much progress, I still needed to rely on the kindness of others during hectic times and *yomim tovim*. Before I knew it, Pesach arrived and my family spent a wonderful *yom tov* at the home of friends. Since I love being around people, I truly enjoyed all the company. Here's a journal entry I wrote right after *yom tov*.

April 11, 2007

> All in all, Pesach was enjoyable and a big success. There is no comparison to last year, when I was still in the hospital and terribly depressed. I had a week off from all my different therapies and exercises, and now I have to get back into it. I'm feeling refreshed and quite ready to jump right into routine. I hope to see some significant progress in the near future. Now that Pesach has passed, I have plenty of time to spend on my recovery.
>
> This afternoon I went to the supermarket with Kasia and the children. I pushed Shloimy in the stroller, and Kasia pushed Libby in the shopping cart. We spent about an hour and a half shopping

and restocking our home. This was the longest shopping I have done, and I managed pretty well. I was good and ready to sit down by the time we arrived at the car, but I didn't get fatigued too quickly.

There was more excitement in store that month, since my brother-in-law's wedding was scheduled for the middle of April at the same hall where both my brothers had gotten married. Once again, I saw the progress I had made. I had a much easier time in the bathroom stalls and was even able to walk upstairs with my quad cane for pictures. It was wonderful to see my husband's entire family who had flown in from overseas, and I was able to enjoy this *simchah* much more.

Since it was too hard to attend any of the *sheva berachos*, I decided to make one myself. I planned the menu, shopped for paper goods and ingredients and directed Kasia while she did the actual cooking. Since we did not have enough room in our house for all the guests, the Ehrmanns kindly offered to host the event.

Boruch hashem, the *sheva berachos* was a big success. The tables looked beautiful and the food was delicious. We had a nice crowd of mostly family members and the atmosphere was truly enjoyable.

When I came home after the *sheva berachos*, I decided to finish a good book that I had been reading. I had stopped wearing an eye patch in public for some time already, but I continued to wear one at home to help me focus when I read. I was reluctant to waste a new eye patch for such a short

One Year Post-Op

time, and since my vision had improved slightly, I decided to try to read without the patch. I kept losing the place, but I finished the book nonetheless.

The next morning, I decided not to put on a patch and see if I could manage. It was only slightly uncomfortable. Thus, I resolved to say goodbye to the eye patches at last and hoped that my eyes would coordinate quickly.

April 26, 2007

> I am glad to report 'it just keeps getting better and better.' As of three days ago, I stopped wearing the patch altogether. I have noticed that my eyes are improving at a much faster rate than before. I am able to read comfortably without it now. My vision is still double when I look to the left and slightly double to the right. When I look straight ahead, I can see much better, but not perfectly.
>
> Today was the second time I went walking in a park with Shloimy in a stroller. There is a park nearby that has a paved walking path that goes around a pond. The total length of the full circle is one third of a mile. When the weather became nice, I decided to try to walk there. I went a couple of days ago and saw that it was absolutely doable. Kasia timed it for me; it took about eighteen minutes. Today when I went, it took fifteen minutes. I hope to go walking there three times a week from now on.

STRUGGLE TO THE SUMMIT

This morning I showered and dressed completely by myself. Yesterday Samantha was here, and though her specialty is physical therapy, she helped me work out different techniques to be able to do each task according to my current abilities.

Until now, I wasn't ready emotionally to even give it a try. I wasn't willing to accept having to do things in a "not normal" way. My husband kept telling me that doing things this way first would eventually help me do it the regular way. I argued that once my hands work correctly and I can walk properly, I would just be able to do things normally. I finally see that he is correct and feel ready to try. The more I use my hands, even in a clumsy way, the better their dexterity becomes, and I will soon be able to do things normally. I am even using the sock aides I said I would never use. At last I can get them without help and put the socks on them myself. I finally see their value and am happily using them.

I also plan to try to drive again in the near future. I tried once last fall and felt that my coordination was not good enough then. It's more than six months later, and I am much better. I think I might be ready.

Every evening after my children have had their baths and are in pajamas, I sit on the recliner, and they both climb up on my lap. We sing and play hand games like "open shut them" or "the Itsy

One Year Post-Op

Bitsy Spider." Then we say Shema and they drink their bedtime bottles while still on my lap. A few days ago, I asked Kasia to give me the hairbrush and ponytail holder. I decided to try to make Shloimy's hair. I managed to make a ponytail, though it did not come out very neat. I did it three times so far, and it is becoming neater each time.

Over the last couple of weeks, I have noticed an overall improvement in almost everything. My left hand seems to have become more capable, I feel steadier, my vision has improved and my writing became a little faster.

My in-laws remember:

Dearest Rivkah,

When you and Sroli first told us about your condition, we had little idea what the future would hold. You did not make much of it to minimize our worries. Even so, knowing that you were heading for serious brain surgery with no immediate kinfolk around was enough. You were so brave. Nobody but you knows what you endured. It was only when I (Mummy) came to visit from England, when you had been in rehabilitation for a few weeks, that I got the picture (or nearly) of your situation. There you were, with your left and right sides almost useless. Doing therapy wasn't easy. Asking the nurses and visitors when you needed anything was so stressful. Not being able to see your precious children, so hard. Life was challenging, so distant - the end of the tunnel, almost unreachable. It pained me to see you, when I knew there was little I could contribute to the situation, and I'm so far away most of the year. You were so lonely most of the time, yet you persevered.

Even when you came home we worried about you, your progress, and the help you needed for everything, besides the care of the children. It was so so sad to think about your situation, especially knowing you were so house-proud and efficient as well as a conscientious mother and wife. You had to tolerate others doing jobs differently than the way you liked, and the orderliness was compromised too.

I admired the way you treated your helpers. They themselves did not realize that it was harder for you on the receiving end than it was for them. It was a blessing that your speech was clear enough so that you could communicate with your children. You were amazing! Zeldy, who was a newlywed, inexperienced cook, gained from your culinary expertise as well as other spheres.

I admired, too, your positive attitude and your determination to beat the odds. You tried everything you could: the way you practiced writing and walking and how you worked on your coordination. How it improved by playing games was a lesson for us all. You had faith in Hashem and drew your strength from that. It wasn't easy.

Gradually, we sensed that those tears which you had shed in the rehabilitation hospital were being replaced by humor and goodwill as you progressed. It seemed so slow to us, but for you, it was still going forward. You were always grateful to anyone who helped you, even if the person was hired. Most of all, your faithful husband who stood by you and encouraged you forward, through thick and thin. You knew we cared, so you were so thoughtful in keeping us in the know about your progress.

Your children will not remember what you went through, but hopefully they will inherit your resilience, which will help them in their future. May you have continued nachas from them and go mechayil el chayil.

Our love always,
Daddy and Mummy

15
Spring 2007

*I*n the beginning of May 2007, I diapered and dressed Libby completely by myself for the first time. I changed her while standing at the changing table and dressed her while I sat on the recliner and she stood on the floor in front of me. It was not too complicated, especially since she could help me as I dressed her. Then she sat on my lap so I could put on her shoes and socks. Her socks were loose, but I knew that tighter socks or tights would have been too hard for me. I also tried dressing Shloimy, but it was much more difficult. Due to the fact that he is young, he cannot help me and also runs away.

May 3, 2007

    Shloimy was very cranky this morning and kept saying, "wanna goya ow-side." Since I have been walking in the park with the stroller for almost two *weeks, I felt confident enough to walk with him outside by myself. Kasia put him in the stroller, and I walked with him up and down the driveway for about twenty minutes.*

I have been making Shloimy's ponytail for almost a week, and the fingers on my left hand are learning to move properly to complete this task. I am also able to gather all his hair together with my left hand, which I couldn't do last week.

The tasks I just mentioned are ordinary ones that mothers normally take for granted. Being able to do them brought me a great deal of joy. I am happy that I have reached this point and am able to do some normal mothering activities.

One of the challenges of changing Libby's diapers was that I had to stand while balancing and using my hands. I had been standing at the sink to brush my teeth and wash my hands for a while already, but I had always leaned against the sink for support.

Seeing that I could do this, I decided to try something new again. On Shabbos morning, I asked someone to bring the oil and vinegar to the counter near the spice cabinet. I stood at the counter and seasoned the salad that the girls had made. Later, in the afternoon, I changed Libby's diapers while standing at the changing table again, and the next morning I dressed Shloimy while standing as well. I still had to lean a little on the changing table to maintain my balance, but I knew that the more I would do it, the easier it would become.

Spring 2007

May 15, 2007

I feel that recently I have made great strides in many areas, and I am truly pleased with my progress. Since I no longer wear an eye patch, I feel more normal. My sight is good, except that I still see double to my left. Therefore, I request that people not talk to me while standing or sitting at that side. I still have numbness in my left hand and around that side of my mouth. I think the lack of sensation in my hand is hindering its capabilities. In addition, my left arm feels weighed down. Although I can lift it up completely, the force of gravity is very strong, and I cannot hold it up for long. I have full range of movement in my left hand as well, but my hand resists, and I can only move it slowly. I hope that just as my eyes are getting better without extra therapies, the numbness will also disappear and my left hand will become more functional.

I wrote the following poem yesterday. It shows my current physical status and my confidence in becoming completely well real soon.

I'm getting there,
And on the way.
I just get better,
Day by day.
I can dress my baby,
At the changing table,
And I'm quite surprised,
That I am able.
My morning routine,
I'm on my own.
I do it myself,
I do it alone.
And with my kids
I've formed,

STRUGGLE TO THE SUMMIT

A real strong bond,
We interact a lot,
In ways of which
   they are fond.
As they sit on my lap,
We play and we sing.
Then I read them
   some books,
The ones which they bring.
My wheelchair's gone,
It's away in the shed.
And it's getting
   easier to move,
At night in my bed.
With my son in his stroller,
I walk on the path
And I make his hair
   each night,
After his bath.
There's not a moment
   to waste,
No time to just sit.
I'm getting back to myself,
With time, bit by bit.
It's a lot of hard work,
There's so much to do.
My therapies are many,
But I'll name just a few.

There's the pool and
   Manhattan,
And my exercise in bed,
And coordination exercises,
For the brain in my head.
The patch on my eye,
I don't wear anymore.
But I still need the brace,
Cause my ankle's still poor.
I walk with a quad cane,
On which I've learned
   to depend.
I can't do without it,
So now it's my friend.
It's a matter of time,
Until I am well.
I hope it is soon,
Time will just have to tell.
I've kind of grown used to
Things how they are.
But I know to keep working
To come up to par.
At the rate things are going,
It shouldn't be long.
Until I'm back to myself,
All healthy and strong.

Shavuos was at the end of May, and we spent a pleasant, uneventful *yom tov* at the Ehrmann's house. The first anniversary of the day I had come home from the hospital was a few days later. I had progressed tremendously since then. Of course, I had hoped that by this time I would be completely better, but that was not the case. I just had to look back and see how far I had come and look to the future with the hope of achieving my long-term goal of complete recovery.

The Ehrmann's daughter Pessy was the one who arranged for girls to come each Shabbos to help me when Kasia was not around. They took care of the children, set the table, served, cleaned up and even loaded the dishwasher after Shabbos. I was so grateful each week for the girls who came so willingly to spend Shabbos with us, knowing they would hardly have a moment to relax. I know we would not have managed without their help. To express my appreciation I wrote the following poem, which was then placed in a frame on the night table in the room where they slept.

To my dear helpers,

This is not so easy
For me to express
But there is one thing
I have to address
And that is gratitude
For your eager support
Without which I
* wouldn't manage*
To keep up my fort

You change diapers,
* set the table*
And serve all the food
You entertain and
* take care of*
My little brood
You came here for Shabbos
With a smile on your face
Not to rest or relax
But to work in my place
You do all my tasks
Readily and with zest

STRUGGLE TO THE SUMMIT

Like my home is your own
And you are no guest
I can't tell you how much
You're doing for me
You make the atmosphere so nice
For my whole family
You do what I can't
With your hands and your feet
And I give you my orders
While I sit in my seat
I want you to know

That I value your work
That you graciously do
Without any perk
My appreciation for your help
I proclaim and I state
May Hashem repay you
For this chessed so great

With great appreciation,
Rivkah Zucker

After some time, we started inviting family and friends (instead of girls) to spend Shabbos with us. It was a positive change. We were finally able to enjoy the company of couples we knew, while they helped us run our home and care for the children over Shabbos.

Shortly after Shavuos, on June 1st, I went out with my husband to see if I was ready to drive. When I had last tried nine months earlier, my reflexes had been too slow. I also still had severe double vision then. In addition, my left hand was uncoordinated, and it was difficult to turn the steering wheel. After that driving attempt, my husband had installed a steering wheel spinner knob that allows the driver to safely and easily steer the car with only one hand.

This time, when I sat into the driver's seat, I felt more capable. Although my double vision had not disappeared completely, I could see well enough to drive. I noticed that

Spring 2007

I still needed practice controlling the car and staying in the center of the lane. My judgment when turning corners was not so good either. My left hand had not improved much, but the spinner made turning easy for me. I just had to get used to the feel of turning with it. I realized that my turns were too wide, and I turned past the street I was going into. I practiced on unpopulated side streets and took it slowly and carefully.

At around the same time, I decided to finally toilet train Libby, who would be turning three in a month. Until then, when people asked me about it, I joked, "Either she will train herself, or she will have to wait until I am better."

Now, she kept getting awful diaper rashes, and I knew I could not delay it any longer. She seemed enthusiastic, and though I could not take care of the physical aspect, I was able to talk to her and encourage her. I soon realized that a large part of mothering is how one talks to the children, because while Kasia performed all the necessary tasks, I was actually the one doing the mothering.

June 7, 2007

> I am glad I can finally cover my hair properly. I had shaved it almost entirely when I couldn't take care of it during the early stages of my recovery, and it had given me a hard time once it started growing back. For a long time, quite a bit would stick out at the back of my neck, and I wore a shaitel, which did a better job at covering it than a snood. Eventually, I started wearing a snood all the time again, which is much more convenient.

I'm really glad that I can finally wear one without any hair sticking out.

Today I drove with Kasia and Shloimy to Wal-Mart, then to the supermarket and finally back home. I actually felt comfortable being behind the wheel. My driving has gotten much better since last week. I went out driving with Kasia yesterday for about fifteen minutes. I still don't stop smoothly or turn corners too well, but I am staying in the lanes. From now on I plan to do all the local driving.

I also saw this morning that I have the stamina to run more than one errand at a time. Not too long ago, I would go to one store and that was enough for me for the day. This morning, I was out running around for almost two hours!

By mid-June, I was doing all the local driving. I saw a tremendous improvement from when I first started a couple of weeks earlier. I felt much more in control and was quite confident at the wheel. My turns and stops also became much smoother. I did not feel ready to try highways, though, since I first had to perfect my local driving. I still focused too much on my own driving, and it was difficult to concentrate on what was going on around me.

I think driving was a good therapy for my eyes, since it forced me to look in all directions. Until then, I had avoided looking to my left, since it was so uncomfortable. I still saw double in my left field of vision, but it had improved since I started driving.

Spring 2007

My therapy schedule was still quite rigorous, although I did cut back on some things. I stopped doing leg exercises in bed in the morning in order to give more time to my children. While we were downstairs at the breakfast table, I continued writing and circling the word finds with my left hand every day. I improved in the control and coordination of my left hand, but it still needed more perfecting.

I no longer played games during the morning hours. Two mornings a week I went to the pool for water therapy, and I used the other mornings for running errands.

Once the weather became hot and humid, I stopped walking in the park. I also discontinued my evening arm exercises and instead used that time to put on Shloimy's pajamas. However, I started another upper body exercise that Robbie showed me, and I continued using the arm pedal and clothespins. I performed these exercises while the children were being bathed, and afterwards we all went on the recliner for stories and Mommy time.

I continued to play games from eight to nine o'clock every night. This activity served several functions. It was a social outlet which helped me improve my fine motor skills. It also prevented me from being alone after Kasia left and my husband was learning with his *chavrusah*.

I went to Robbie Ofir once a week and to water therapy twice a week. By now, I saw Samantha only once a month, since I no longer needed physical therapy on a regular basis.

I started standing at the kitchen counter to make a vegetable salad every Shabbos. When I stood, I had to consciously shift my weight to the left; otherwise, my right leg bore the brunt of all my body weight. One morning after I brushed my teeth, I noticed that there were footmarks on the plush bath rug I had been standing on. I had not distributed my weight evenly, and the mark from my right foot was noticeably deeper than the mark from my left foot. I knew I would have to continue focusing on this.

June 27, 2007

> *From time to time, people ask me if I plan to become a therapist when I am better. My answer is always no. I want nothing more than to become a full time mother. I can't wait to cook and clean, do laundry, dishes and all the other mundane tasks housewives do. I do want to help people going through a debilitating illness, but nothing on a professional level. I know what worked for me and what I hated doing, so my advice or support might be helpful to others. I also came up with several fine motor activities that helped me, and I learned how to keep busy in only one place.*

Towards the end of June, I tried putting on my socks without the sock aid one morning. Though I had to position myself just so on my glider, I discovered that I was able to do this. At around the same time, I also started taking some pictures and video clips of my children. I was only able to hold a camera while sitting, so most pictures were views of my children at the kitchen table. I noticed that my hand was much steadier than it had been only a few months earlier.

Spring 2007

By now I had realized that there would no longer be any major milestones. However, as I steadily noticed improvements in every area, I knew that while the climb up the mountain was slow, I was certainly covering ground and making significant progress.

A sister-in-law remembers:

Dear Rivkah,

Before I was engaged, your brother Yehuda Hillel told me that he felt extremely close to you. In fact, he told me that you were close to all your siblings and were very involved in all their lives. You were a big doer, so capable and geshikt. You cooked, baked, sewed and gardened. You always organized family functions.

Then, on my third date, I learned about your brain surgery and condition. Yehuda Hillel was deeply upset about it. He had depended on you for support, and you had suddenly lost all of your capabilities. He was devastated. After we became engaged, he brought me to meet you. The first time I saw you, you were sitting on a recliner, with a patch on your eye, unable to do the most basic things. I tried to envision you as the capable person my new chasan had described. It was hard to imagine.

Eery time I see you, I see progress. You are always doing better than the previous time. I've spent quite a few Shabbosos at your house. The first couple of times I came, you had help in the house. When you started doing things like setting and serving yourself, you declined my offer to help. You told me it was therapy for you, and you wanted to do as much as you could by yourself. I admire your strength and perseverance and the way you persistently push yourself to improve.

As time passes, I see more and more of the true you. I really see the traits Yehuda Hillel first described to me. I only daven and hope for you to have a complete recovery. I feel proud to be your sister in-law.

Love,
Devorah Mirel

16
Summer 2007

July 3, 2007

Kasia will be leaving in about four weeks. I am not so concerned, since we've had a good track record until now. Hashem always sent along just the right person to help me. I am only concerned about my children's reaction. They have become strongly attached to Kasia and will feel abandoned when she leaves. Of course I will be there running the show, but I think they will be upset.

I hope to find someone new who will start a week before Kasia leaves, so she can train her in. My new helper will not have to drive, since I do all the driving now. I still don't drive on highways, but I hope to do so in a few weeks. Since the new helper will have to go into the pool with me, she will have to come along to observe what Kasia *does with me in the water. I am not as anxious as I was last time we looked for someone. Now I'm more capable than I was a short time ago.*

Lately, Libby only wants me to dress her and put on her pajamas every day. I help her while I'm sitting down. She can actually get dressed by herself. I hold her clothes in a good position for her to get into. Since I am dressing her, I don't dress Shloimy anymore. It is still too much for me to do both. Libby also gets excited when I drive. I think she is happy when I do normal things. It means a lot to her to have a functioning mother.

In the first week of July, I drove on the highway for the first time. I felt comfortable and in control. There was not too much traffic, so it was fairly easy. I even tried switching lanes a few times and this did not pose a problem.

July 7, 2007

Libby turned three last week and Shloimy just turned two. My children are getting older, and I enjoy watching them and spending time with them immensely. I sometimes sit outside on the patio with them when they play outside or splash in the wading pool.

July 16, 2007

I have to write about this, since it's been on my mind all day. This morning in Scenic View, I met a woman who seems to be in her fifties. She was using a walker with wheels that has a seat attached to it. Her walking was uncoordinated and clumsy. I started talking to her, and she was friendly, chatty and upbeat. I asked her what she was coming to therapy for, and she related her condition to me; a degenerative neurological disorder. I immediately wished I had not asked. She has a devastating disease which can paralyze a person and sometimes leaves them a prisoner in a dysfunctional body. In truth, I had little encouragement to offer her.

If strangers would have seen us without knowing our conditions, I would seem to be much worse off, since I am in a wheelchair. However, I am well on my way to recovery. Unfortunately, her condition is degenerative, and she is moving in the opposite direction. As for myself, my future looks promising. I have much to look forward to. Of course, I was as encouraging as I could be and wished her well, but I was left with an extremely unsettled and depressed feeling.

I have so much for which to be thankful. As hard as my situation is, I have to thank Hashem that it is only temporary. There are so many worse situations than I am in, and I am enormously grateful for my lot.

July 22, 2007

A week has passed already without me having anything significant to report. Things *are constantly getting better. I feel steadier and more stable all the time, but I haven't had any specific breakthrough I can pinpoint. I compare it to someone who is watching a clock. He barely notices the minute hand moving, but he sees after some time that the minute hand has advanced quite a bit. I feel it's the same way with my progress; it's a slow moving process, and I can only pinpoint milestones after some time has passed.*

July 25, 2007

This morning I tried to shower while standing for the first time. I was pleasantly surprised that it was not too difficult. I still cannot take any steps without holding on, so I remained in one place most of the time. When I had to take some steps, I used the grab bar on the wall for support.

By the end of July, I had started assisting with some food preparation while standing at the kitchen counter. I cut vegetables for salads and occasionally prepared green beans and braided *challos*. I stood mostly in one place and took a few steps with the support of the counter when I moved. After about ten minutes I got pins and needles in my feet, because I did not move them around enough.

At the end of July, I changed my children's bedtime routine. Until then, they slept in separate rooms, and we spent pre-bedtime together downstairs on the recliner. I decided it was time for Libby to sleep in a bed, and I moved Shloimy to her crib in the same room. I asked Kasia to bring in the glider chair, and bedtime went without a hitch, as I sat on it while reading and singing to them in their bedroom.

One day, Kasia and I visited a medical supply store to purchase a new cane. I had been using a wide base quad cane and no longer needed that much support. The saleslady first showed me a narrow base quad cane, but after watching me try it, she said I did not need that either. In the end, I bought a regular straight cane with a tripod base. I had never seen or heard of a tripod base before. It is a rubber piece that is triangular shaped with the corners flattened. It gives a bit more support than the straight cane alone and keeps the cane upright when not in use.

I happily put my quad cane into retirement. My new tripod cane is so lightweight that going up and down stairs became much faster and easier. I was a little concerned about walking on non-level surfaces, but I soon realized it was actually easier than with the quad cane. A straight cane has one point of contact with the ground and can be held upright on any surface. A quad cane, however, has four feet, which made it unstable for me on non-level ground. I was delighted about this new development. It was a step in the right direction.

Kasia was scheduled to return to Poland at the beginning of August. Several days earlier our new helper, Iwona (pronounced E-Vona) arrived. Kasia showed her around during her last three days with us. Iwona was cute and petite with long straight honey colored hair. She was also from Poland and was twenty-one years old. Iwona did not speak English well, but we were not concerned, since the language issue had worked out well with Dorothy. We hired her to live-in and work for us full time. She planned to stay with us all week and go to her relatives for Shabbos.

I had prepared my children well for this change. Libby understood that Kasia had to leave, and I needed a new helper. Shloimy is an easily adaptable child and given that he saw that Libby was all right with the change, he was okay as well. Since I was managing the bedtime routine almost completely by myself, it was an easier adjustment for them.

My husband was distrustful of Iwona and told me to be cautious with her. Since his intuition about people is usually correct, I promised to keep my eyes open.

At first, I was satisfied but wary with Iwona. She seemed to develop a good rapport with the children and said that she liked to cook and clean. Iwona used the same recipe notebook Dorothy had started. Kasia had added the dishes and recipes that had not been there yet before giving it to Iwona.

Though Iwona did not drive, this was not a problem, especially since my driving skills had improved significantly. Dr. Ofir was out of the country, and my next appointment would not be for another couple of weeks. I hoped I would be ready to drive to Manhattan by then.

Summer 2007

August 4, 2007

I wrote the following poem which expresses my feelings of how I view myself as a mother. This new phase is a direct result of having a new helper and making some positive changes in how my household is run.

I finally feel
Like a mother once more
To my two precious children,
Whom I so adore.
Although there's a lot,
I still cannot do.
That doesn't matter,
From my kids' point of view.
To them I'm just Mommy,
The way I should be,
They don't know any better,
My flaws they don't see.
I make booboos better,
With a hug and a kiss.
It works really well
'Cause innocence is bliss.
When bedtime arrives,
Only Mommy will do.
No one's as good,
To them, this is true.
When they want a nice treat,
They come and ask me.
I am their mother,
It's simple you see.
They sure can sense it,
They feel and they know,
I am their mother,
And love them just so.
I may not be doing,
The physical part.
But mothering I am
And I do that with my heart.

August 6, 2007

I'm afraid my husband's intuition might be correct. Yesterday morning, Iwona came back from *her future sister-in-law after spending the weekend with her. She bathed the children in the morning, as I like to do on Sundays. We had a rather productive day with her accompanying me and the children to a cousin's upsherin party, organizing the pantry together and cooking supper. At around six thirty, after supper, Iwona went upstairs to her room. I heard her talking angrily on her cell phone and crying. I don't understand Polish, but I knew it had nothing to do with me as we had a pleasant day together.*

When seven o'clock rolled around and it was bedtime for my children, I called her name, but she did not respond. I decided to go upstairs with my children. I figured she would hear us and come to help. I called her name again with no response. Since my kids had been bathed in the morning, they just needed to change into pajamas. Their pajamas were out already from the previous night, and I managed to change them myself and put them to bed.

When my husband came home a short time later, I told him what was going on. He went upstairs to Iwona's room and knocked on her door. She came to the door still on her telephone with tears streaming down her face. She told my husband that she would come down shortly and explain.

At nine thirty, all was quiet, but she did not come downstairs. My husband then called her cell phone. She said that she is having problems with her family and is already in bed for the night.

I went to bed with my head spinning. I felt profoundly let down and betrayed. I was afraid we would have to find someone new and disrupt my children again. Children become insecure with inconsistency, and I know I cannot manage without reliable help. Should we immediately start looking for someone new or try to make this work?

I had a very troubled night, and this morning, when Iwona came to my room, I asked her what happened. "I know, I'm sorry," she said. "It won't happen again."

At breakfast, she told me she is not getting along with her future sister in-law. They got into a big fight over the weekend, and she does not want to go back to her. She then asked me if she could stay here for some weekends when she cannot go to her friend.

I could not believe my good fortune! Finding girls each week for Shabbos has not been easy, and if she could stay here, it will really be helpful. I decided that we should give her a chance. I told her she could stay for every Shabbos if she would like.

One day in August, while I was driving Libby to day camp, she asked, "Mommy, are you going to water therapy after you drop me off?"

"Not today," I replied. "I go twice a week, but today is not a day that I go."

"I want you to go every day," she said.

"Why?" I wondered.

"I want you to walk without a cane," Libby explained.

Libby is a smart little girl and understood that exercising and going to therapy was necessary for my recovery. I was deeply moved by her longing for me to get better.

A few days later, Libby asked me to buy her a little cane. She accepted my cane as a fact of life, and since children like to emulate their parents, she wanted a cane to be like me.

After Iwona came, I spent much more time downstairs during the day, since we'd given her the room where the computer was kept. Now, I used a laptop computer downstairs on the kitchen table and was able to interact and supervise my children much more. I was also more involved with cooking, adjusting the flame and supervising Iwona.

August 16, 2007

I feel great! I just kneaded the challah dough by hand. My sister was here and helped me; she assembled all the ingredients and added the flour as I needed it. I used my right hand to do the kneading and stood at the table, which is just the right height for kneading dough. This is something I dreamed about doing and thought was far off in the future. Today I decided to give it a try and I succeeded.

Summer 2007

At the end of August, I finally visited Robbie Ofir again. About six weeks had passed since my last appointment. First, he had been out of the country for a month, and then I had waited for my husband to drive with me on a trial run to see if I could make it safely on my own to Manhattan. My husband was satisfied with my driving abilities, so I planned to drive myself with Iwona accompanying me for all my future appointments.

The drive to Manhattan was just one example of the many ways I was taking control of my life. I was much busier these days with household responsibilities and spent less time on therapy regimens, such as writing each morning. Even cooking, which was physically done by Iwona, was ultimately supervised by me. If something was overcooked or not seasoned properly, it was my fault and not hers.

Though I still had many limitations, I felt much better overall. My eyesight, though still not perfect, was much improved and my speech was almost back to normal. Only when I spoke for a long time and became fatigued did my speech became slightly slower, making me feel as though I was tripping on some words. Nonetheless, the speech impairment was so slight that it was hardly noticeable. In addition, after a long time of not having enough strength to project my voice, I was able to sing again. I had practiced while singing for my children at bedtime, and I could finally sing with ease.

As the end of summer approached, I began planning the menus and cooking for *yom tov*. It felt wonderful to be so completely in control of my household again.

Reuven Ofir, Ph.D., P.T., CFT

Re: Rivkah Zucker:

I am so delighted and honored to have been given the opportunity to work with Rivkah.

From the first day I met her (January of 2007) in my studio when she came in with a wheelchair, assisted by her aide, I was struck by her easy optimism, her keen intelligence, and her fierce independence.
I looked at a young woman, a mother of two very young children who had undergone a life threatening brainstem surgery that had left her with severe physical disability manifested in double vision, left sided paresis including compromised sensation, barely functioning left upper extremity and severe gait disturbance, yet what I saw were her flashing eyes, her easy smile and determination to do whatever it would take to regain her independence in all domains of her life particularly as a caring mother a loving wife, and a contributing member of society.

Rivkah has done wonders for herself. She's a poster woman for the unlimited capacity of human beings to improve and grow. She demonstrated and continues to demonstrate in her daily life all that Moshe Feldenkrais conceived of and applied in practice over sixty years ago in the method that bears his name – concepts that have been confirmed by the revolution in brain studies over the past 25 years as described in Dr. Norman Doige's book: "The Brain that Changes Itself".

During the two years I have known and worked with her, Rivkah has progressed from a woman barely able to walk, often needing to use a wheelchair, using her right arm almost exclusively, dependent on an aide for most of her daily activities to driving independently, running her household on her own, doting on her children, walking independently with a straight cane and using her left upper extremity appropriately when needed (She is right handed). Not only has she taken full active responsibility for her long road to full rehabilitation, but has taken upon herself the Mitzvot of helping others who are less able or less fortunate than herself.
Rivkah still has a road to travel and I have no doubt she will achieve all she has set her mind to do.
Of Rivkah it is said "A woman of valor who shall find..."

With respect and Affection,

Reuven (Robbie) Ofir
Feb. 2009

159 West 53 street, New York, NY 10019
Ph: 212 265 6591 E-Mail: robofir@aol.com
Also: 5055 Collins Ave. Miami Beach, FL 33140 Ph: 305 868 4961

Letter from Dr. Reuven Ofir

17
Fall 2007

September 1, 2007

It is Motzei Shabbos, and I decided to load the milchig dishwasher. The fleishig one is on the left side of the sink, so it is too hard for me to load, but the milchig one is on the right side, and I can load it by just rotating my torso a little, without having to move my feet. I wanted to give it a try. I asked my husband to put everything that was meant to go in the dishwasher from Shabbos into the sink and to fill the detergent compartment. I loaded it and turned on the wash cycle. The feeling was amazing! It's incredible how such an ordinary thing caused me to feel so productive and happy.

September 4th was the first day of playgroup for my children. Unlike the previous year when I was wheelchair bound, I was able to go into the classroom with both of them. What a wonderful feeling!

I recalled how emotional I had been a year ago, crying at home when Libby went off to playgroup. I worried that I would have the same reaction when it was Shloimy's turn to start. Since my brain surgery, I cannot always control my emotions. At times I laugh uncontrollably at something that is not even so funny, and sometimes I find myself weeping over something that does not actually warrant tears. This bothers me immensely; I hope to regain a grip on my emotions before long. In the meantime, I sometimes have to deal with embarrassing episodes. Luckily, though, on this particular morning I was so busy concentrating on my walking that I had no time to contemplate the significance of the occasion and become weepy.

With both kids in school, I had more time on my hands. I was able to focus completely on *yom tov* preparations. Iwona and I spent the children's first day of school shopping for groceries and other items.

Around this time, a few things about Iwona started to trouble me. First, I no longer felt comfortable trusting her, since she had lied to me on more than one occasion. For instance, once after the children were in bed, I noticed the smell of cigarette smoke emanating from her bedroom. I knocked on her door, and it took about a full minute for her to respond. She finally opened it a crack and stuck her head out.

"Why are you smoking in the house?" I asked her.

"I am not smoking," she answered. "I know you do not like it."

"Why are you lying to me?" I asked, upset. "Can I come into your room?"

She reluctantly agreed, and when I walked in, it was clear that she had been smoking. Besides the smell that hung in the air, her window was wide open and a box of cigarettes was lying open on the desk. She still denied having smoked and I could not believe her audacity. How could she lie straight to my face like that?

"I don't believe you," I told her, "and if I ever even think you are smoking inside the house again, I will look for a new worker."

She looked at me with a straight face, feigning innocence. I made myself clear but did not mention the subject to her again afterwards.

This incident was one of a few that showed Iwona's dishonesty. In addition, she also became a little lazy and sloppy. She bought herself a laptop computer and tried to cut corners so she could go to her room sooner. I noticed some laundry put away inside out and shopping bags left in the car overnight. Whenever I brought these things to her attention, she responded with a shrug and did not truly seem to care.

September 20, 2007

Yesterday, Iwona upset me again. It was in the evening after supper and almost bath time. Iwona wanted to empty the dishwasher and the kids wanted to "help." Iwona kept telling them not to touch. I told her to wait until they were in bed to put the dishes away. Iwona just kept trying and ignored what I had said. I had to tell her three times until she finally listened. Later I confronted her about this and she replied, "I just wanted to get it done."

"The children are out of the house most of the day and go to bed fairly early," I told her. "You should not unload the dishes during the short time they are around. There are sharp knives that are dangerous, and the kids always like to touch. It's not fair to put temptation in front of them and then get annoyed when they act like children."

Later I had a discussion with my husband about the future with Iwona. He wants to look for someone new. I feel like I have a teenager around, the way she just does her own thing even when I tell her otherwise. My husband does not trust her with the kashrus. Also, people who lie tend to steal as well, so we have to be cautious. I told my husband we should wait until after Sukkos because we need her for the Shabbosos over yom tov. It is exceedingly difficult to find help for an entire week.

This morning she disappointed me again. Iwona knows I like to participate when the kids get dressed in the morning, but she dressed them when I was still in the shower.

"Why didn't you wait for me?" I asked her.

"I wanted to save time," she answered with a sheepish smile.

"I get pleasure from choosing their clothes," I explained, "and it's not fair to take away the time I spend with my children."

I don't know what the future with Iwona will be. I am keeping my eyes open and trying to be very firm with her. I'm an easygoing boss, but I do know how to give instructions. In order for my home to run the way I would do things myself, I have to be explicit and demanding.

My husband and I decided to try to make it work out with Iwona. She planned to stay until late January, which was not so far away, and except for her dishonesty, she was an excellent worker. She interacted well with my children and truly seemed to like them. I also enjoyed working side by side with her in the kitchen; she cleaned well and was very efficient. I just knew to be on constant guard and make myself extremely clear. I had to be very specific in my expectations when I gave her instructions.

Once we decided we would stick it out, I became much friendlier to her. As a result, she was more receptive to my requests.

Though the situation was not perfect, I was glad things had settled down with Iwona just in time for *yom tov*. Thus, Rosh Hashanah and Yom Kippur passed pleasantly enough and as Sukkos approached, I looked forward to spending the time with my family at home.

STRUGGLE TO THE SUMMIT

September 25, 2007

The time Iwona and I spent on food preparation for the last few weeks was well worthwhile. Most of our Sukkos food is ready in the freezer, and we only have a few more dishes to prepare. Today we worked as a team while making schnitzel; Iwona pounded and breaded the schnitzel, and I stood at the stove and fried them. By the time I finished, my feet felt like they were on fire from having stood in one spot for so long. As painful as it was, I didn't mind. I was just so happy to be cooking.

A while ago, I had a conversation with Libby about my condition. "I am getting better," I told her, "and when I am better, I will do all the things we have a helper for."

I told her a list of things that I will do, including cooking. When Libby saw me standing at the stove frying the schnitzel, she asked me excitedly, "Mommy, you're better!?"

September 26, 2007

Someone made a comment to me last night, and I've been stewing over it ever since. I am sure she has absolutely no idea that her words were hurtful, and in fact, she absolutely meant to give me chizuk.

Last night, my husband and I made a surprise visit to someone. As today is Erev Sukkos, they were very busy with all kinds of last minute *preparations.* My husband proudly commented how we were basically finished and all ready for yom tov. I explained how I have to get everything done during the day. Iwona goes up to her room around seven in the evening, and I cannot do anything on my own.

"I'm sure you're really able to do everything," the woman said.

"No," I answered her, "I still cannot do most things on my own."

She argued with me and tried to tell me how I truly am able. It's half a day later and all night I turned it over and analyzed it in my mind to understand why this comment disturbed me so much. I have concluded that her comment implies that I am actually able to do things, but I choose not to.

It is difficult for others to be consciously aware of my limitations, while they continue with their daily lives, taking their mobility and abilities for granted. It soothes people's conscience when they think I truly am better, and when they comment on my wellbeing, it makes it seem more a reality in their minds.

Another thing occurs when people question my physical wellbeing. I generally dwell on what and how I can accomplish things and not so much on my disability and what I am unable to do. When people inquire as to how I am managing, it causes me to verbalize and think about my deficits. I usually answer people, "I'm doing fine; you have to wait for my book to get the details."

It's just too hard for me to explain. People ask out of sincere concern, and they have no idea how just merely asking can be troublesome for me.

In truth, I show a facade of being better. People see me going shopping and hear how I'm boruch Hashem coping well. My children are always neat and clean; my house is organized and well run. Therefore, they tend to think I am better, although my abilities are actually still quite limited.

Aside from small non-delicate items, I still cannot really carry anything from place to place. I use my right hand which has better coordination to hold the cane. My left hand is still quite weak and heavy, so it's hard for me to hold it up. I recently carried a drink from the counter to the table for myself. I used a plastic cup and only partially filled it. I still spilled some along the way because I had to use my left hand. I also cannot carry anything on a plate because I am unable to hold the plate straight. The most I can carry is a fruit, the telephone or a paper.

A couple of weeks ago, I tried to dice an onion. I was only able to do half. Once there was only a small piece remaining, I could not grasp it with my left hand anymore. I was also unable to cut very small pieces.

Fall 2007

>Last week, I wanted to cook farfel by myself. Iwona prepared everything on the counter for me. When I cut the bag of farfel open, I ended up spilling some on the counter. My left hand was too clumsy to hold the farfel bag steady.
>
>I am constantly trying to be more involved in food preparation, but I usually end up making a mess. Iwona understands and just cleans it up, but I still feel uncomfortable about it.
>
>I still have a hard time cutting my food. I usually eat with my left hand resting on my lap. That's the most comfortable place for it. When I try to involve it, I find that it just gets in the way.
>
>I would be lying to say my limitations don't bother me, but I am not bitter about them either. I see constant improvement, and I always imagine myself fully functional. I daven every day, asking Hashem to restore my function. I know with time He will do so. I just have to be patient and persevere. I have to learn to ignore hurtful comments. I know they are unintentional. People just cannot fully understand what I am going through and want to make me feel better.

Sukkos passed and it was a beautiful, enjoyable *yom tov*. We had guests, and I truly enjoyed the company. Iwona stayed for the Shabbosos throughout *yom tov* and kept the house in perfect order. She set the table, warmed the food, cleared up after the meals and took care of the children.

My guests also pitched in during the *seudos*. I felt a little awkward sitting the whole time as my guests served me, but everyone understood and did what had to be done.

Our *sukkah* was located on the patio right outside our house. It had a sliding door that lined up with the kitchen door. To get into our *sukkah*, I had to step over the tracks from both the house door and the *sukkah* door. Last year, this had been exceedingly difficult for me, and Samantha had shown me how to get into the *sukkah* by walking sideways and stepping over the door tracks. I was not that steady yet and had to hold onto the wall as my husband stood behind me. Even then, it was quite challenging, and I washed for *hamotzi* in the *sukkah* with a cup and basin that my husband brought me. This year, I was much steadier and able to get my foot up and over the tracks. I held on to the door handle to steady myself, but I did not need the assistance of another person. I went back into the house as needed to instruct those who were serving the food.

Time and again, these little triumphs showed me how far I had already come. They encouraged me to hope that, with time, I would reach even greater milestones.

Mrs. Udi W. remembers:

Dearest Rivkalah,

I was so excited to read the manuscript of the book you've been working on for so long. I feel like your book cannot be appreciated and your pain after the surgery cannot be truly felt if your readers don't know some background information about who you are and how you led your life before this bombshell hit you.

We have known Sroli, your husband, for many years. We love him dearly and he is part of our family. We were so happy when he introduced us to you, his wonderful kallah and later when we watched you begin to build your bayis ne'eman.

Rivkalah, when you had your children in quick succession within the first two years after your wedding, we never worried whether you would be able to care for two babies. You could manage anything. Your house was always in perfect order, and you were one of those people who could prepare an entire sheva berachos in a matter of hours.

Rivkalah, not only did we marvel at your geshiktkeit and competence, but you were also truly a one-of-a-kind mother. All mothers give of themselves selflessly for their children, but you simply had no self where your children were concerned. When the welfare of your child was at stake, you completed disregarded your own needs.

I remember one Rosh Hashanah, when we had invited your family to eat the seudah with us. After a long, exhausting day in shul, everyone was tired, hungry and eager to settle down for the meal. We had only just washed when Libby, the baby, started kvetching. You explained that she was due for her nap and said that Libby would not sleep well in a strange crib. Without any hesitation, you and Sroli, who hadn't even started to eat, picked yourselves up and walked the twenty-minute walk home to put Libby to sleep.

Another time, when our Betzalel was going to be Bar mitzvah, you said you would bring along your camera and take pictures for us (since you take beautiful pictures). We were counting on you. On the night of the bar mitzvah, Libby was sick. You wouldn't leave her with a babysitter. In the end, Sroli missed the bar mitzvah and stayed home with the baby, so that you could attend and take the pictures as you had said you would.

In fact, from the day Libby was born, she and then her brother were constantly with one of you. You never left your children in the care of anyone until...

When you woke up from the surgery with all those disabilities, no pain was stronger than the separation from those babies. The tears didn't stop. You must have cried rivers of tears, oh to be with them again. No wonder. Such a mother!! A mother par excellence, one in a million.

Boruch Hashem, you are where you are today. We couldn't bear to watch your pain, and now, we delight in your being together enjoying their toddler years, b'simcha uv'tov leivov.

Hazoirim b'dimah, b'rina yiktzoiru.

Furthermore, as far as Sroli goes, he has been a bulwark of strength, kindness, devotion and emuna and bitochon-being mechazeik us all, like the real eved Hashem that we always knew he was.

Looking forward to reading the finished version and shepping nachas from you and Sroli.

With much admiration,
Mrs. Udi W.

18

Winter 2007-2008

During one of my sessions with Robbie Ofir in October, I told him how the weakness in my left arm handicaps me greatly. In response, Robbie told me to lie on my right side and extend my left arm straight up to the ceiling. Then he told me to move my hand slightly to the left and right while keeping my elbow in a fixed position. Afterwards, he told me to move my hand up and down and draw small circles. Throughout these exercises, I had extremely poor control, and my hand and arm just jerked and flopped in big, out-of-control movements. Robbie assured me that with practice I would gain better control of my arm. He gave me a variety of exercises to perform with my arm, including writing my name in the air.

October 14, 2007

    This morning I drove to Manhattan to see Dr. Ofir. The West Side Highway, which I usually take, was closed due to a bicycle event, and I had to take a different route. The road was crowded from traffic overload, and a traffic light at every street corner backed everything up even more. I have never driven this way before, and I didn't know the way. I called Robbie and he directed me to an alternate route. Three more times I had to detour because of road closure due to construction or a street fair. I managed to navigate in the crowded Manhattan traffic with confidence and without getting lost. I feel like I passed the real driving test! I know people who don't drive in Manhattan at all, and I managed alone even with my disability.

Iwona told me this morning that she will probably have to go back to Poland in a few weeks. Her mother has a medical problem, and she feels that her place is at home. She is working out okay now, but I won't miss her too much when she leaves. However, I'm not looking forward to the hassle of finding someone new.

In October, I started going to the Wellness Center at Scenic View Rehab Center three times a week. The Wellness Center is a gym geared to people with disabilities, and the exercise is supervised. I truly enjoyed it, and with this added activity, my days were now full. I went to the center on Monday, Wednesday and Friday mornings. On Mondays and Wednesdays I went to the pool following my exercise session and only came home around two o'clock. On Fridays, I went to pick up my children from pre-school immediately after exercising. I left all my shopping and errands for

Winter 2007-2008

Tuesdays and Thursdays and continued seeing Robbie Ofir in Manhattan on Sunday mornings. I truly enjoyed my full days after being so immobile and bored for such a long time. Iwona accompanied me wherever I went, to carry my things and assist me when needed. She still had to get all the housework and cooking done in between, and we had to pick up the kids at four o'clock each day. I also baked *challah* every other week, kneading the dough by hand and braiding the *challos* myself. My life was hectic and I loved it.

Although I loved the new routine, I soon had to adjust to some changes when Iwona left on November 7. Before leaving, she put a classified ad on a Polish website and helped us find our new helper, Mary. Mary was about sixty years old and had come from Poland to work for a year or two. Although I preferred someone young like Dorothy, Kasia and Iwona, I could not afford to be choosy.

Mary had some knowledge of Shabbos and *kashrus* from a previous job and spoke and understood basic English. She was interested in staying for at least a year and wanted to go away for only one Shabbos a month, which was ideal for us.

Though my children were well prepared for Iwona's departure, they were not too happy with this change. Iwona had really connected well with my kids, and while Mary was okay, it was just not the same. I was compelled to involve myself more with their care than before. Even though it was challenging, I was happy.

November 7, 2007

    Yesterday was Mary's first day here alone without Iwona. Until now I showered in the morning and walked to the children's room only after I was dressed and wearing my brace and shoes. I decided to begin showering at night and go directly to their room when I wake up. It was the longest walk I have taken so far while barefoot, without wearing the brace. It was hard, but I managed. I just didn't feel comfortable leaving Mary to deal with the kids alone on her first day here.

At bath time yesterday, I sat in the bathroom to oversee the bathing. Until now, Iwona would take the kids upstairs and bathe them. I would only go upstairs when they were coming out of the tub. With Mary here, I'm much more involved at mealtime as well. Iwona used to feed the kids when they would dilly-dally over their food. At last, it is my job to make sure they eat up. As hard as it is having a new aide, I realize that each new helper brings me the opportunity to take on more responsibility.

Shloimy was deeply attached to Iwona and misses her terribly. He constantly asks for her and says, "I want Iwona to come back!"

I know with time he will forget, but I feel bad that it is so hard for him. Libby, on the other hand, doesn't seem to care too much about this change; she liked Iwona but only wanted me for comfort.

After Mary had been with us for about two weeks, I was satisfied with the way things were turning out. She worked efficiently with me in the kitchen and did all the housekeeping on schedule without letting it pile up. We went together to buy outerwear and Shabbos clothes for Libby. Shopping with her was a pleasurable easy experience.

While Shloimy slowly started to accept Mary, Libby refused to call her by name. Instead, she would tell me that "the lady" did this or that. She also insisted that I accompany her to the bathroom and buckle or unbuckle her car seat. She became quite naughty, hitting and biting Mary and scribbling on the floor. I figured it was her way of protesting the changes and hoped that within a few weeks she would adjust. She was usually such a well-behaved child, but she had never done well with change. I assumed that this development was the source of her behavior.

November 27, 2007

> Last week I prepared the challah dough almost completely by myself. I retrieved the bowl from the cabinet, measured the water, sugar and yeast. I took the eggs from the refrigerator, and cracked and checked them. I needed help with the salt, since you need two working hands to measure, one hand to hold the spoon and one to pour. Then Mary carried the bowl to the table and added the flour as I kneaded the dough. Once it had risen, she brought it back to the counter for me. I divided the dough, rolled out the strands and braided the challos myself.
>
> Since Mary came, I have been the one to wash my children's hands for netilas yadayim each

morning. The kids know to pull a chair to the sink and climb up. I take the washing cup, fill it and wash their hands. I also wash their hands with soap and water when they come home from school. I love the normal motherly interaction I am able to finally have.

The last time I went to Dr. Ofir, he suggested that I walk backwards on the treadmill on the slowest speed. I tried it yesterday at the Wellness Center at Scenic View and it was fascinating. It wasn't too hard to do, but I noticed that I tend to drag my left foot a little; I have to consciously pick it up. I plan to do this every time I exercise, and I hope to see some improvement in my walking. Yesterday someone saw me after not having seen me in a while. She said I was walking much faster than the last time she saw me, so I know my exercise pays off.

Libby has really settled down. I am working with her with prize charts, which are quite effective. At this time, Shloimy is Mary's friend and Libby started calling her by name. We have passed the trial period with Mary, and boruch Hashem, I am satisfied with her.

December 20, 2007

This is the longest stretch as yet for me, without having anything that significant to report. I've been steadily doing exercise three times a week at the Wellness Center at Scenic View; my driving has become second nature; and I just live my life and supervise the running of my home with the capabilities I do have.

Chanukah was last week. I went shopping for gifts and wrapped them together with Mary. Last year I just asked Dorothy to do it. This year I stood at the table and actually did some of the wrapping myself. I also stood at the stove and fried the latkes, which was unthinkable last year.

Every year my family has a Chanukah get-together. This year it was at my brother's house, which is located a few miles away from mine. Shloimy was too tired and had to go to bed, so he stayed home with Mary. My husband came straight from work. I went alone with Libby, and my brother came outside to meet us and help me into the house. Last year there was no choice but to have it in my home. It was much too difficult for me to get to and from the car and to be in places that were not handicapped accessible.

My children had a few days off from school, and I figured it was a good time to finally visit a friend of mine who lives in Lakewood. I've been promising to visit her for a long time. The drive is between one-and-a-half and two hours, with most of the time spent on a busy highway. I've been driving back and forth to Manhattan for four months already, so I figured I was up to it.

A friend in Lakewood arranged a small get-together of about ten high-school classmates. It was truly enjoyable seeing some old friends again. The drive was uneventful, and my children had a good time. I feel like I'm finally getting back into the swing of things!

December 23, 2007

I am compelled to mention some nitty gritty details of my day-to-day function, because I feel so appreciative in being able to accomplish these small tasks.

For about six weeks now, since Mary came to us, I started to make my hair on my own. At night after I shower, I make my ponytail and put on my snood. I can only do this when my hair is wet and clumps together easily. Though it is still not easy and doesn't come out perfectly, I can accomplish it on my own and that's a major milestone for me.

Oranges are now in season, and I buy them all the time. I can finally peel them myself. Last year I didn't buy them often. I didn't like bothering someone to prepare it for me each time I wanted one.

In general, I started doing more small food preparation like making hot cocoa for my kids on cold, snowy mornings or cooking them oatmeal for breakfast. I started to make them grilled cheese sandwiches or pasta for lunch. I can finally carry items that aren't heavy. When making the grilled cheese sandwiches, it takes me three trips to get *the bread, ketchup and cheese, but I manage myself. I assemble the sandwiches on the counter right in front of the toaster oven, so they don't need to be carried anywhere. When they are ready, I put them onto plates, and my kids carry them to the table. With the pasta, I can do everything myself until it is ready and needs to be drained. Then I need Mary to finish it up for me.*

I started filling the kids' drink bottles as well. I use the counter near the refrigerator so I don't have to carry the heavy juice bottle if it's full. I use a funnel so I don't spill, and my kids come to me to get their drinks. I put in a great deal of effort to do as much as I am able without calling Mary to help me.

In January, a few issues with Mary disturbed my husband and me, so we decided to try to find someone else. Firstly, I did not know whether she was hard of hearing or always jumping to conclusions about what I was saying. I explained things until I was blue in the face, and she still did them incorrectly. I was also not happy about how she related and spoke to my children, and it was clear that they did not like her either. Unless they were sleeping, I really felt uncomfortable leaving them with her.

One evening I went to the bathroom during suppertime and heard Shloimy crying. Mary had put a scorching bowl of soup on the table in front of him. He touched it, and she yelled at him not to. *Boruch* Hashem he had not gotten burned, but I was simply afraid to leave the room for even a few minutes because of her lack of common sense when dealing with young children.

One Friday, Shloimy had to bring the Shabbos party to school for his class. On Thursday evening, I prepared a bag of lollipops on the kitchen counter, so we would not forget to send them to school the next morning. On Friday, when I came downstairs, both children were licking lollipops.

"What's going on?" I asked Mary.

"They wanted it," she replied.

"Come on!" I exclaimed in exasperation. "You should know not to give it to them. You're an adult, and they are young children."

She shrugged and said, "I don't know. They took them themselves."

The lollipops were ball-shaped with a twisted wrapper, and I knew my kids could not open them by themselves. I asked them who had opened them, and they told me Mary had. There was no catastrophic result of this incident, but I was quite annoyed at her indifference and lack of judgment.

There were some other incidents that annoyed me. Once I tried to explain patiently my reason for a specific method. Mary shrugged and said, "If you don't like my work, find someone else."

January 15, 2008

> My husband bought me a utility cart, so I can move things around the kitchen. The other day I wanted to bake cookies with my children. I was able to move the cart around the kitchen, load all

the ingredients I needed and bring it to the counter where the mixer is. Instead of a cookbook, I use my laptop which has all my recipes stored on it. I set it up on the table and enlarged the font so I can read it from across the kitchen. My husband had purchased a cookie scooper for me so I could make cookies with one hand. I cracked and checked the eggs and prepared the cookie dough myself. I needed Mary to put the cookies in and remove them from the oven. The experience of baking cookies with my children standing on either side of me was thrilling. It felt so normal.

In middle of January, I prepared the chicken for Shabbos mostly unassisted. My balance was so much better that I felt steady enough doing things while standing. Mary assembled everything I needed at the sink. I could not clean the chicken as well as I would have liked, but I knew with time and practice I would get better at it.

Grapefruits were in season, and I have always loved the freshly squeezed juice. I had a hand citrus juicer in the house and decided to try it out. Since the juicer was easy to use, I started making myself freshly squeezed grapefruit juice almost every day.

For a long time I had been unable to clean up and organize the toys. Therefore, I did not want to have many toys with little pieces around. It really bothered me when there was a big jumble of different toys mixed together, and I dreamed of the day that I would be able to organize it properly. Over Chanukah, my kids received little cars, blocks and doll dishes, adding to their previous collection of Lego, puzzles, books and a variety of bigger toys. I decided to buy containers for everything. Then I sat with Mary in the playroom and sorted everything. I designated a specific place and container for each toy.

Once the playroom was organized, I supervised a complete clean up every Motzei Shabbos with Mary and the kids. Every evening before bedtime, we would quickly clean-up. Afterwards, I would reward them by playing a game together.

I had not had much opportunity to change Shloimy's diaper since Mary came. During the morning and bedtime routine, I always dressed Libby while Mary dressed Shloimy. At six o'clock one morning, Shloimy came to my room and said he wanted Mary to change his diaper. I did not want to wake her so early and decided to do it myself. I went to his room and lifted him onto the changing table. Changing him and closing his snaps was much easier than it had been only a few months earlier. Even though I had woken up earlier than usual, I felt immense pleasure that I had been able to change him.

About three months had passed since I had started exercising at the Wellness Center, and my endurance had increased tremendously. I had been walking backwards on the treadmill for about a month, and it became much smoother than when I had started. As a coordination exercise, I walked with one foot directly in front of the other, heel to toe, on the treadmill at the slowest speed. When I first started doing this, it was difficult to position my feet in the right place. Now I could place my foot in the right spot every time.

Winter 2007-2008

January 23, 2007

Feeling ecstatic from all the things I started doing, I wrote the following poem.

The pleasure of doing
Normal things,
Even when it's hard -
The enjoyment it brings
I've baked challos
   and cookies
and juice freshly squeezed
Mostly myself,
And I'm feeling
   quite pleased.
I prepared Shabbos chicken
No easy task,
But I did it myself
What more can I ask?
My home is in order,
Everything's in its place,
Of the fact that I'm
   not perfect,
There isn't a trace.
And I diapered my son,
When it was still early morn'
And pleasure I felt,
Like when he was just born.
I am still quite limited
In what I can do
But I'm doing a lot
From my point of view.
The elation I feel
When I manage a task
Is too exciting for me,
For my feelings to mask.
But I must thank Hashem
For making me heal,
For giving me strength
And helping me deal.

At the end of January, I cracked my brace slightly while going down the stairs. Subsequently, I was able to fully flex my ankle and extend my toes. I saw that my ankle was strong enough to get by without the extra support and decided it was time to give up my brace. However, sometimes I dragged my left foot, which caused me to stumble, or my ankle bent sideways, which resulted in a near fall. I decided to see if an old pair of hi-top ankle boots would help, and to my satisfaction, they did the trick and supported my ankle. I called them my baby shoes because babies often start walking with high tops. Though I had to walk a bit slower, I managed fairly well without my brace.

At the end of January, I started using my utility cart on Friday nights to serve the *gefilta* fish and dips. I prepared them in the kitchen, loaded them onto the cart and brought it to the dining room. I also set the Shabbos table for the first time. I loaded everything onto the cart and then wheeled it over to the table. I used it to unload the clean dishes from the dishwasher and put everything away as well.

January 29, 2008

> *I am becoming more and more functional in the kitchen, and I am thrilled! Besides the cart, there are a few other changes in my kitchen. I've always stored a large bottle of oil under the kitchen sink. Now I keep a small, easy-to-manage size on the counter next to the stove. Mary refills it from the large one under whenever necessary. Last week I put a large gallon sized container with a shopping bag in it onto the counter, and I use this as a garbage can while I work. With these new conveniences, I no longer leave a mess when I prepare food at the counter.*
>
> *I also recently bought two ceramic canisters, one for parve and one for fleishig, in which I keep all my spatulas, large spoons and ladles on each side of the stove. My cooking utensils are now more easily accessible.*

Winter 2007-2008

I did not go to the Wellness Center and pool last week. On Monday they were closed, and on Wednesday I was feeling under the weather. On Friday I didn't have time since Mary was going away for Shabbos and had to finish her work before she left. Besides not feeling so well, I had a wonderful week. I baked knishes, pineapple pies, cupcakes and challos, all mostly myself. It was a week spent doing all kinds of domestic things and nothing involving therapy. Usually my week revolves around my exercise and therapy schedule, but last week I was a regular homemaker. It felt great!

Since I came home from the hospital, I've been getting a manicure every other week. I am still unable to cut my nails myself, so it's a necessity. In the beginning, I barely used my hands and the polish pretty much stayed intact for the entire time. Over time, the polish chipped on my right hand, and my left hand stayed nice. The last time I had them done, the nails on both hands chipped in under a week. I finally use both hands for cooking and washing. I've decided it's time for me to stop using nail polish.

We have been becoming increasingly unhappy with Mary, so we really have to find someone new. In the meantime, I am constantly making progress and becoming more functional, so the job description keeps changing.

February 12, 2008

In two days, it will be two full years from my surgery. I am so used to being disabled; I can hardly remember what being "normal" is. Of course I still long to be better, but I am at the stage where it is not a constant thought. I am living in the present and not in the future.

Some friends see me as better since I am functioning. They think I should end my book here. I, however, insist that when I won't need any more help to do ordinary things - it will be time to conclude. I have not reached the top of the mountain yet. Maybe I'm three quarters of the way there. I think I can almost see the top, and when I get there, I will finally share my story. In the meantime, my friends will have to be patient as I work hard to recover, so my story continues...

My husband remembers:

During her recovery, Rivkah often asked me how we were paying for her aides, therapy, special equipment and the other numerous expenses related to her care. I didn't want to worry her and always replied, "Hashem provides." In truth, it was no simple matter. This was one of the many challenges I struggled with at the time. Boruch hashem we owned our own home, and eventually I took out a $150,000 equity loan to help cover our many expenses.

When Rivkah and I were in Arizona, I asked Dr. Spetzler what to expect post surgery. "It's hard to say," he told me then. "Some patients remain in a wheelchair forever; others can walk a bit, and still others lead almost normal lives."

At the time, it was difficult for me to understand how there can be such varied results. Later, I was able to appreciate how much lies in the hands of the patient. I have no doubt that not many people in Rivkah's situation would even be walking yet, forget about doing the myriad tasks that she has learned to do on her own. It was only her determination and resolve that allowed her to make such strides during her recovery.

My wife is truly an unbelievable person. Her willpower and mind-over-matter attitude are truly astounding.

She exhibits such strength and self-discipline on a daily basis that all those around her are awed and inspired. She is adamant about fully recuperating. She constantly looks for new therapies that will facilitate her recovery and products that will increase her independence.

19
Two Years Post-Op

Purim of 2008 was the third Purim I celebrated since my surgery. This time I was the driver and went around with my husband and children to deliver *mishloach manos*. I fashioned a *kallah* costume for Libby using a glue gun. I decorated it with synthetic flowers, a string of plastic pearls and tulle. It came out really nice, and I thoroughly enjoyed making it. Libby paraded around all Purim with a happy smile on her face.

After Purim, my husband and I visited Dr. Schick in his home. He was the neurologist who first saw me and diagnosed my condition. My husband had remained in touch with him throughout, constantly updating him on my progress. Because my case was so unusual, he had a special interest in it. Dr. Schick was impressed with how far I had advanced, and although I was using a cane, he said I was walking quite well. The last time he had seen me walking was before the surgery and my gait had been uncoordinated and clumsy.

We discussed the different therapies and exercises I was doing. Dr. Schick suggested that I try to learn something new. He explained that he also advises his Alzheimer patients to do so, because when new skills and information are acquired, new channels open up in the brain and promote healing.

It was a pleasant and informal visit that we all enjoyed. We left with the intention to keep in touch in the future.

After the visit with Dr. Schick, I decided to take his advice and began learning to type with one hand. I had learned to type in high school, but now, with limited use of my left hand, I was unable to type correctly. I did some research on the Internet and found a one-handed typing manual that was written by a woman who had lost most of one hand in an accident as a young child. I purchased the manual and bought typing instructor software to practice the drills. I learned it pretty well, but I had a hard time with the shift and number keys. Although I never mastered one hand typing, I was still learning a new skill. I do not know whether it was a coincidence or a direct result, but I started to improve at a greater speed thereafter.

Around this time, I started to take some steps around my kitchen without using the cane. I noticed that I had a very pronounced weight shift from side to side, as I walked. I asked Robbie how to get rid of it. He taught me how to lift up my pelvis with each step I took, so I would not have to lean so much to get clearance from the floor. I was amazed how such a minute movement caused such a difference.

Two Years Post-Op

At the end of March, I finally decided I had had enough of Mary. My husband sat down with her to discuss her future with us. She told him that she was returning to Poland in two weeks. I could not believe that she had been planning to leave and had not said a word about it until we approached her. Nonetheless, I was grateful that I had two weeks to find someone and that Mary was leaving of her own accord without any hard feelings.

As always, it was stressful looking for a new aide. I immediately placed an ad on the same Polish job website as Iwona had used. I had many responses, but most callers were not suitable for us. Finally, I received a call from a twenty-year-old girl named Dildora from Tajikistan. She came for an interview, and we agreed to hire her.

Dildora was tall and thin, with an attractive Asian face. She seemed fine and intelligent and had a good command of the English language. As with previous helpers, I had Dildora and Mary overlap each other for a few days to ease the transition.

Dildora started working for us at the beginning of April. She communicated quite well and had a nice rapport with the children. She had depth and intelligence, and I was happy to have her as my new companion.

On her first night alone with us, I saw that Dildora had no idea how to bathe children and wash their hair. I decided to try bathing them myself. My poor balance prevented me from sitting on the edge of the tub, so I went down on my knees on the floor instead. The tiles were much too hard, so I asked Dildora to fold a large towel and place it on the floor as a cushion. At first, this position was hard for me, and I was unable to reach for anything without falling over. Dildora assisted by handing me things that I needed. With time, my balance improved and I could manage without her help. It felt unreal and exhilarating to be bathing my children again.

Since Dildora's arrival, I also changed how I managed the laundry. Dildora did the laundry only once, and though Mary had shown her how to do it, I sensed that she really did not know how to sort the clothes or when to put things in the dryer. I did not have the patience to teach her and was itching to do it myself. I asked Dildora to bring all the laundry to the laundry room, and from there I was on my own. As each load came out of the dryer, I called Dildora to take it away. I cannot begin to express how much satisfaction I had from doing laundry.

At first, my husband was annoyed that he was paying a pretty penny for live-in help, and I still chose to do the laundry on my own. After just a few times doing laundry, I realized how beneficial this chore was for me. I had to bend in various awkward positions as I sorted clothes and reached into the washer and dryer. Within a short time, my balance and mobility improved, and I attributed much of my progress to doing the laundry.

Pesach was coming and not having visited my in-laws for three years, we made plans to travel to England. I looked forward to spending time with my husband's family, and I was happy my children would get to know some of their cousins. I felt ready to travel, but I knew we would not manage without extra help. My children were young and still needed constant supervision, which I was unable to provide. I also knew it would be too much for my husband to help me, keep an eye on the kids and carry the luggage all on his own. Thus, I

Two Years Post-Op

asked my cousin Rivky, who had helped me so much in the hospital, to come with us for Pesach. She was glad to have the opportunity to take a trip to England with all expenses paid and agreed immediately. It was wonderful having her with us for the whole trip, and I was able to relax and enjoy Pesach with her assistance.

Before the trip, I was concerned about how I would manage without a grab bar in the shower. I purchased one from a catalog that suctions to any smooth surface. It was a lifesaver, and I was able to shower safely in my in-law's home.

Another important item I packed was my makeup mirror. I usually applied my makeup while sitting in front of the mirror, since it was too hard for me to balance while standing and using my hand. I did not have a table for the mirror in my room, however, and I felt uncomfortable putting on makeup at a table in front of everyone. I decided to try applying makeup while standing in front of the large wardrobe, which had full-length mirrored doors. I managed to do so during my entire stay in England. During our return trip, the mirror broke, so from then on I stood in front of the mirror. In the beginning, it was a little difficult doing the finer lines, but with time it became easier.

We came back from England on May 1, and I resumed my exercise at the Wellness Center after having been away for two weeks. I discovered that I was able to walk backwards on the treadmill much better than before. I also decided to try the elliptical trainer. I had tried it periodically, but each time my left knee would lock backwards in mid stride. This time, I was finally able to do it. I started using the elliptical trainer for five minutes each time and my movements became smoother.

I also started some new exercises in aqua therapy. The pool had three depths: two feet and nine inches, four feet and five feet. I had been walking in the four-foot water all along and it was not difficult for me. I decided to try the shallower water. It only came up to my waist, which was perfect therapy for my upper body. At first, it was difficult, but it became easier to walk there after only two times.

Another exercise I started was squatting all the way down in the shallow water while holding onto the railing. Out of the water, I could not squat lower than a regular sitting position without experience intense pain. My muscles were not accustomed to that position, and it was almost impossible to reach anything in the back of a bottom cabinet.

Once I started squatting in the pool, I was able to squat outside of it too. I started practicing out of the water holding onto something for balance. Then I tried without support, testing to see how long I could last without falling. My balance improved, and it was not long before I was able to clean up a spill on the floor while squatting.

Shortly after coming home from England, my cane became a nuisance in the kitchen. I realized I was holding it in my left hand to free up my right hand for carrying things. I started leaving it propped up on a counter, but it would constantly fall and be in the way. Finally, in June, I stopped using it in the house. I asked Robbie Ofir if it was a wise decision or too premature. "It's okay now," he assured me. "Your walking pattern is regular enough, so you won't learn bad walking habits."

Two Years Post-Op

Soon after we returned from England, I started toilet training Shloimy because he would soon be turning three. He was well prepared for the big step and this time, I was the one who took him to the bathroom when he needed to go. He was fully trained within two weeks, and it was a real accomplishment for him as well as for me.

As I learned to manage more tasks efficiently, I became brave about putting things into the oven and removing them when they were ready. I always put the food on the cart and wheeled it right up to the open oven door. This eliminated all carrying, and I simply had to transfer the pan from one surface to another. I stood to the left side of the oven door and managed quite well like this. Unless it was really necessary, I did not preheat the oven.

I also started peeling vegetables and cleaning chickens on my own. I found that kitchen shears were the easiest tool for me when I prepared chicken. I had always used a knife in the past. I peeled carrots, parsnips and cucumbers, though I still left apples and potatoes for Dildora. Because of their shape, those foods were still too difficult for me to grasp.

Though things had worked out well with Dildora at first, problems began developing after Shavuos when she began asserting herself about how things should be run in my home. She repeatedly voiced her opinion on various matters. When I specified how I wanted something done, she would respond, "What's the difference?" When I once asked her to find a paper, she asked, "Why do you need it?"

Dildora also spent an awful lot of time "doing laundry" upstairs in her room. When I asked her to fold laundry on the dining room table, she was not too happy. "Why do I have to?" she asked.

About once a week, Dildora would wake up late, even though she was supposed to help me with the children in the morning. By now, I was capable of getting the children ready on my own, but Shloimy often became tangled in his clothes when he tried getting dressed by himself. I would ask him to come to me so that I could help him, but he would run away crying in frustration. Since I could not run after him, I needed Dildora to help me.

Dildora's lateness really upset me. I would be sitting in the children's room wasting my time as I waited for her. She was also frequently late at the Wellness Center in returning when I needed her. She would apologize each time, but her attitude showed that she really did not care.

I was also disturbed when Dildora began interfering with my mothering. Shloimy grew attached to her and at night, when he refused to go to bed, he would say, "I'm going to Dildora." In addition, sometimes when he cried after I punished him, she would pick him up and comfort him.

Dildora also became lazy and did not keep the house so clean anymore. Once when we came home from a shopping trip with the children, she brought in the packages and disappeared, leaving everything on the kitchen floor. Before I knew it, Shloimy emptied a whole box of zip-lock bags. I called Dildora, and when she finally came, I asked her where she had been. "I was resting," she replied nonchalantly.

That was one of the final straws. I seriously considered letting her go. That night I had a discussion with my husband

Two Years Post-Op

about all the issues I had with her. We discussed my current needs for assistance and decided that I would start preparing for independence.

My children were both in playgroup until June 20th and it was located in a house with a steep uneven driveway. There was no way for me to get them to and from the classroom without help. Once the school year was over, however, I believed that I could figure out how to manage every aspect of my life without assistance.

One of the things I still needed help with, for example, was transporting my things to and from the pool for water therapy. I searched on the Internet and found a cart that resembles a baby stroller and is meant specifically for carrying packages. I ordered it and solved that problem.

I started doing dishes and loading and unloading the dishwasher on a regular basis. I tried as much as possible to do things without asking Dildora for help. When we went grocery shopping, I put everything in the cart and unloaded it onto the counter. Dildora was surprised with the changes that were taking place and questioned me about it. "I need to learn to do as much as possible on my own," I told her.

Before, Dildora provided an extra pair of hands when I gave my kids breakfast and supper. Now, I tried not to call her down at mealtime and to manage everything on my own. The most efficient way to manage meals was to put everything we needed on the cart and have it handy near the table. This way I did not have to get up in middle of the meal for salt, ketchup, drinks and other items.

As the school year came to a close, I felt ready to manage on my own. On the last *Motzei Shabbos* in June, when my husband picked Dildora up from the train station, he explained that I was capable enough and he could no longer afford to continue paying for full-time help. Dildora understood and agreed to leave at the end of the week.

I was euphoric and happily anticipated being completely in charge of my home again. I was not worried about how I would manage. I had every last detail worked out in my mind and felt ready to take the plunge.

A frequent visitor remembers:

Dear Rivkah

It's hard to believe it will soon be three years since we have met. I'll never forget the first time I came to visit you. It was the Thursday right after Purim. I had no idea what your condition was and walked into your room feeling anxious and unsure of what to say. You were sitting in a wheelchair with a patch covering one of your eyes. Although your speech was slurred, you were very friendly and upbeat. Looking around your room, you had different signs hanging, each with an inspirational quote or a Chazal on emunah and bitachon. I was amazed. This was one small glimpse of what you are and what your life personifies.

When I came back the next week, you explained your signs and gave ideas on how to learn from them. You were the one giving me chizuk. From then on, I would anticipate coming to visit you. I would get so excited whenever Zehava Pearl would call me and ask if I was available. At first, it was once a week, then it became twice or three times a week. I always left Scenic View amazed and inspired at your tremendous determination and perseverance.

You were so determined to do anything to help yourself get better. Whether it was in the morning, afternoon or evening, your mood was always the same:

happy and cheerful. You were always looking at the bright side of things. You only focused on your future. There were never complaints, only acceptance of your matzav. You did anything that came your way that could involve some practice skills. You never gave up. You were always trying and trying, whether or not you succeeded.

Whenever we played games or did the jigsaw puzzle and it took a long time to pick up pieces, you kept trying and didn't give up. It was your unbelievable determination and willpower that kept you going. I was so excited for you when you were finally discharged from Scenic View. I remember you were nervous about how you would manage at home, but everything boruch hashem went well.

Later, I visited you at your house to schmooze and play games. You were always buying new games and trying to do therapy for yourself while playing them. Of course, you always won! Whenever I came over, you always updated me on your latest progress, even though it was minimal. You were always so excited to share the news. You were so accepting of your limits and came to terms with your matzav very well.

As I watch you run the show in your house, I can only marvel and think, "When there's a will, there's a way!" You are a true example of "yagati umatzasi."

Two Years Post-Op

Hashem should give you siyata dishmaya and determination to persevere and go on, to always accept everything b'ahavah. You should be zocheh to a refuah shleimah bimeheira!! Thank you for everything!

With much admiration,
Raizy

20
Independent at Last

On July 4th Americans celebrate Independence Day. In 2008, July 4th was my personal independence day as well. Dildora was finally leaving! I was well prepared, and I counted down the hours excitedly. At 1:00, I joyfully drove her to the train station.

After Dildora left, I started having cleaning help three times a week. My home was cleaner and more organized than when I had had full time help.

I started sweeping the floor, which was quite tricky at first. My arms were not well coordinated, and I would fling the dirt across the room. With practice my sweeping improved, but since I still could not walk well, it was a hard job for me. My husband bought me a handheld cordless vacuum that I used to pick up the pile of dirt. I did not have the balance yet to use a dustpan.

Another machine I used was a food processor. I use many onions when I cook. Since slicing and dicing were still hard for me, the food processor came in handy.

After Dildora left I felt like a newlywed, playing house in my own kitchen. I would putter around happily until late at night. I used my cart for almost everything. I kept two baskets on the bottom of the cart; one was full of clean *shmatas* and the other was for dirty ones. I also kept a bottle of cleaning spray there.

The feeling of independence was invigorating! I started going to the pool myself, and since I was busier with housework, I stopped playing games in the evenings. After putting my children to bed, I spent my time doing dishes and straightening up. At first, I thought I would continue seeing the volunteers, who had become my friends. I invited them to accompany me during shopping trips. After only a few times, however, I realized that I was capable of managing on my own, and I enjoyed the privacy and solitude.

Shloimy's third birthday and traditional first haircut were at the end of July. Afterwards, it was easier to wash his hair, and I no longer had to make his ponytail.

During the summer, both children attended a backyard day camp around the corner from our house. It worked really well to have them together, so close to home. Though the drive took under a minute, I could not walk on the bumpy ground outdoors yet, so I picked them up with the van.

Both of my children matured quite a bit over the summer. They dressed themselves each morning, even closing their buttons on their own, which was still hard for me to do. They buckled their booster car seats themselves, which was a big help too; I no longer had to walk around the car each time we went out. They also helped me with the laundry, gathering the clothes for me in garbage bags and throwing them down the stairs. Then they went down and dragged the bags into the laundry room.

With all my new responsibilities, it was difficult to continue exercising three times a week. I stopped going to the Wellness Center in August and bought an elliptical trainer, which I used every day. I started with six minutes a day, and then I increased it by one minute each week until I was doing ten minutes a day. An elliptical trainer provides the motion for a correct walking pattern, and I did this exercise to re-pattern my brain. I noticed that my legs grew considerably stronger, and I was able to get up from a sitting position more easily.

In the middle of August, we took our first family vacation. When the children had both been babies, it was too hard, and since I had become disabled, it was no longer possible. Now, I was finally able to visit a place that had not been set up especially for me. We took a trip to Lake George, which is more than three hours from our home, and I did most of the driving on the way there.

At the end of August, I cut my left forefinger. The following morning, I decided to try the method I had learned in therapy of putting on socks with one hand. I was able to do it easily using just my right hand. I remembered struggling and crying when my therapist had taught me how to do it. At that time, my hand had been so uncoordinated that the task was impossible. I smiled as I was once again reminded of just how far I had come.

October 2008

I am finally coming to the end of my book, although my story is not yet finished and I am still on the road of recovery. I still have numerous deficits, but my point is not to write "and they lived happily ever after..." One of my motives in sharing my story is to give chizuk to those going through hardships. I also want to convey to them that they can be happy and productive even if not everything is a hundred percent the way they wish it were.

Way back when I first became disabled, I kept imagining myself all better. I would picture my life as it had been before I became ill. It is currently two-and-a-half years later, and I'm functioning at about 85 percent. That does not mean I am 85 percent better but rather that I am able to accomplish that amount of what I used to be able to do. Nowadays when I picture myself doing different tasks, I imagine myself doing them in a modified way. Two years ago, I never would have dreamed I would be satisfied with accomplishing things in a newly acquired way. I wanted to be my old self and couldn't accept something else. Today I am happy with my new self and no longer mourn my loss.

One thing that frustrates me at times is my walking. At home I have not been using a cane for a few months already, and I feel very independent walking without one. To function at home I need

Independent at Last

my hands free; the cane is a real nuisance. When I am trying to get housework done and need to walk quickly, I don't have the time to concentrate, and I stagger and stumble a lot. I still drag my left foot and the knee locks backward which causes me to walk awkwardly. When I go out, or whenever I am in public, I walk with a cane. When I walk slowly and carefully my gait looks nice and smooth, so people who see me think I am almost completely recovered.

Another problem is my balance, which is still poor. Sometimes I end up rocking forward onto my toes, or I put too much of my weight into my heels. When this happens, it becomes a whole balancing act to evenly distribute my weight and steady myself. I can also easily fall if I step on something with my left foot. Even a small bump on the ground can cause my left ankle to buckle, so I have to be very cautious.

My left hand only functions at about fifty percent. I continue to struggle with the heaviness and slight numbness. Nonetheless, I manage most tasks pretty well.

I will most likely continue going to Robbie Ofir for another year or two. I feel The Feldenkrais Method played the biggest role in my recovery. The Feldenkrais Method is a deep learning experience that speaks directly to the brain and teaches self-awareness that no therapy can accomplish. I also plan to continue going to the pool twice a week for as long as I am able. The water has helped me tremendously, and it is very worthwhile to continue.

   I look forward to finally getting rid of my cane altogether and to be able to walk on terrain that's not level. I want to be able to walk down my driveway to bring in the mail, to carry things up and down the stairs, to dance at a wedding or to walk down the street hand in hand with my child.

   In the meantime, I have another letter to write...

Dear Hashem,

It's been almost two years since I wrote You a letter,
Asking and begging to please make me better.
I was frightened and hopeless in a desperate state,
Afraid of my future, unsure of my fate.
I asked not for riches, nor money, nor wealth,
What I wanted the most was simply my health.
I wanted to function, to be able to do,
Cooking and housework and childcare too
To be normal and able, with every part working,
Coordinated and smooth without any jerking.
Physically functioning, just like in the past,
But I was such a big mess, my problems were vast.
I was unable to balance, my vision was double,
I couldn't move my left side, which only meant trouble.
I was unable to care for my precious two,
Which was the worst part - it made me feel blue.

Independent at Last

But throughout my long nightmare,
You were right by my side,
Holding my hand, joining me for the ride.
You sent the right people to fill all my needs,
People who do all kinds of good deeds.
My perspective is altered, unlike before,
Taking for granted, I don't do anymore.
I appreciate function to the nth degree,
And just to be walking, feels wonderfully free.
For the moment I'm happy, actively fulfilled,
Each milestone I reach makes me totally thrilled.
I'm delighted with the progress I achieved thus far
But the yearning's still there, to be up to par.
It might take a while to get all the way there,
But the thought it won't happen's not even a fear.
I've yet to get there and be fully whole,
But with You at my side, I'll surely reach my goal.

Epilogue

It is currently August 2009, about one year since I have finished writing my story. As time passes, I continue to make progress, so there will always be an updated epilogue. Today, I can shop, carpool, do laundry, take care of my children and do most household tasks. Of course, I still have numerous deficits but I lead a mostly ordinary life.

I'd like to share several noteworthy incidents that have occurred during the past year.

One Thursday morning in November, I went to the freezer in my garage to take out some food for Shabbos. When I opened the freezer, I noticed that some of the food seemed defrosted. I had just put in a fresh batch of meatballs the day before, and everything had seemed fine then. As I felt around to see what was affected, I reached around the top shelf where I had placed the containers of meatballs. Suddenly, I bumped a container labeled "meatball sauce" and knocked it off the shelf. It opened on its way down and sauce spilled all over my clothes, the freezer and the floor.

For a few seconds I just stood there in stunned disbelief, not sure what to do next. Finally, I brought *shmatas* from my laundry room nearby, leaving a trail of meatball sauce from my dripping skirt and saturated shoes. I superficially cleaned up inside the bottom of the freezer so that I could close the door.

I made the trek into my kitchen, leaving another trail behind me. I sat down to clean my shoes. I removed the drenched laces and shuffled to the sink to wash them. Finally, I put the clean laces back in, tied my shoes and was good to go.

By now, I was itching from the sauce that was on my skirt and socks, and the smell of meatballs was tickling my nose. I went upstairs to change and then prepared myself mentally for the job that awaited me in the garage.

I excitedly anticipated cleaning the mess I was going to tackle. I filled a bucket with warm water and some cleaning solution, placed it on my cart and wheeled it into the garage. I pulled rubber gloves onto my hands, took a folding chair and *shmata* and got to work. Sitting on the chair, I managed to clean the whole mess without leaving any evidence of the earlier mishap.

When I finished, I called my husband excitedly on the phone to tell him what I just did. I was so thankful for the spill, because it had shown me that I was capable of cleaning up such a big mess. I actually said the words "Thank you, Hashem," out loud.

Epilogue

A few minutes later, I reached up to the cabinet above my stove where I keep the phonebooks. I took down the directory I was looking for, but it slipped out of my hand and bumped into a drinking glass that was sitting on the counter. The glass fell onto the floor and shattered into thousands of pieces across my entire kitchen floor. I burst into laughter because Hashem had just sent me another gift to show me what I was capable of doing.

A short while later, I arranged a reunion for my high school class. I had been dreaming of doing that for five years. Sometime after my surgery, I had gone to Lakewood, where about ten of us had a mini get-together at a classmate's house. At the time, I was not physically or emotionally ready to see everyone. Now I felt ready and decided to organize a reunion.

Most of my classmates were busy with their growing families, and many of them worked as well. While I was quite busy, too, my schedule was more flexible. A friend in Lakewood sent me an updated class list, and I took it from there. My school was kind enough to allow us the use of their building free of charge, and we scheduled the reunion for the *Motzei Shabbos* before Chanukah. I typed and mailed out invitations, hand addressing each one. I was glad to notice that my writing speed was close to normal and my hand did not get tired from writing. The last invitation came out as neat as the first, and I thoroughly enjoyed the task.

I received a very enthusiastic response and counted down the days. A few friends asked me to speak at the reunion. At first, I was reluctant to speak, since public speaking is not my forte. After giving it more thought, I changed my mind, realizing that I had an obligation to share my experience. I also decided to invite a few teachers with whom I felt a special connection, as well as about twenty other people who were somehow involved in my life.

I spent many hours writing and re-writing my speech, considering every word. The reunion was a great success, and my speech was a real hit. Though nerves caused me to speak a bit too quickly, I was articulate and able to speak clearly throughout.

After the reunion, I was on a high for a while. However, we had several snowstorms in Monsey that winter, and I began getting cabin fever from spending so much time indoors. Although I went out for carpool and therapy, I was afraid to spend any other time on the icy streets because of my impaired balance.

One day I received a catalog in the mail that changed everything. I was flipping through the pages when I saw a cane with a retractable point designed for walking on ice and impacted snow. I promptly ordered it, and from then on, the weather did not stop me from going out anymore.

Shortly after I got my new cane, Macy's advertised a big sale. On the day of the sale, snowfall was predicted, and my kids were off from school. It ended up sleeting most of the day, but since there wasn't much accumulation, I decided to go anyway. To my amusement, I found that Macy's parking lot was deserted, and I was the only customer in the store! I felt wonderful knowing that, despite my disabilities, I still managed an outing with my children when most people chose to stay home.

Epilogue

One night, not long afterward, I sat down at the computer to relax for a few minutes. I had just finished putting my kids to bed and wanted to catch my breath before attending to the day's mess. I was not expecting any company, when surprisingly I heard the doorbell ring. I walk slowly, and it took me a couple of minutes to get to the door.

"Who is it?" I asked.

"Dorothy," was the response.

I could not place the name right away and curiously opened the door. There stood Dorothy with her husband and daughter. She had worked for me two years earlier. They were here from Poland, visiting her brother in New Jersey. She was curious about me, so they traveled in to visit. I invited her in and was quite embarrassed of the mess. There were toys strewn about, the floor needed to be swept, and the dishes were piled up in the sink.

Dorothy had brought along two family albums and told me to sit down. "You look at the pictures with my husband," she said, "and I will clean up." I did not argue with her, and in no time, she put everything back in order. I was deeply grateful.

A couple of months later, in March, I bought an electronic device called Bio-ness to help me walk better. Ever since I had stopped wearing the brace on my left foot, I stumbled when I walked. This was awfully frustrating and slowed me down considerably. With each step, my left foot dragged, and I would trip on it if I was not careful.

The Bio-ness had a sensor in my shoe that sent signals to an apparatus I wore below my knee. The device delivered impulses at just the right time to muscles in my calf. The impulses caused my foot to rise at the correct angle, so I would step without stumbling on my foot.

This incredible device was first introduced to me months earlier by Robbie. He showed me an article in a PT magazine about the Bio-ness and recommended that I look into it. I discovered that since Bio-ness is a relatively new technology and not yet recognized by the AMA, most insurance companies do not cover the cost. In addition, not every person responds to electric stimulation, so I had to go down for an evaluation first. After seeing that my muscle responded well, we waited several more months before deciding to purchase it despite the exorbitant cost. Dr. Ofir believes that not only does the Bio-ness help me on a daily basis, but it will also eventually teach my brain how and when to lift my foot correctly.

Since I got the Bio-ness, walking has become less stressful. I still use a cane when I go out in public or walk on unlevel surfaces. However, I have not used one at home for close to a year. When I go shopping, my feet do not get tired anymore. I do not use the Bio-ness on Shabbos and that's when I notice the contrast between walking with and without it. I still cannot walk at a normal speed, and my balance is still impaired, but I have certainly come a long way.

The remainder of the winter was uneventful. I spent countless hours going through my manuscript, making additions and corrections as I went along. On the day after Tu B'shvat, I celebrated the third anniversary of my surgery. I was still not fully recovered but grateful for everything I could do.

Epilogue

Here and there when strangers see me, they comment on or inquire about why I walk with a cane. "Did you hurt your leg?" they often ask.

Sometimes I tell them, "No, I'm much more talented than that; I had brain surgery."

Once, when I was heading back to the car with my children after doing some shopping, I noticed a woman watching me intently. When I reached the car, she came over and said, "You are a pretty, young woman. It looks like you have something wrong with your back or leg."

"Nothing is wrong with my back or leg," I explained. "I had brain surgery."

Well that stopped her in her tracks! "Oh," she said, "I was thinking that a chiropractor might be good for you."

I know she meant well, and it probably took a great deal of courage for her to come over to me and share her secret, but I thought the entire incident rather amusing.

I recently went somewhere, and as I was walking into the building, a friendly man asked what had happened to me. His expression said, "Poor you," as he assumed that I had gotten hurt. When he learned that I was recovering from brain surgery, he did a complete turnabout. "You're doing great!" he said enthusiastically.

This world is full of people jumping to conclusions. I rarely get offended by their comments. I actually feel a sense of pride as I walk with my cane, for it is testimony to the goodness and greatness of Hashem. It was humbling to be so powerless and helpless and to realize how little control we have over our own lives. In the blink of an eye, everything can change. I am proud of how I learned to accept my situation, and the willpower and determination with which I pursued my goal.

Nonetheless, I recognize that while my attitude was crucial to the progress I have made, I could not have accomplished anything on my own. My experience has changed my relationship with *Hakadosh Boruch Hu;* it has truly helped me realize that it is He who guides and supports me every step of the way. It is only through His help and infinite kindness that I have been able to come this far and discover hidden reservoirs of strength and courage during my journey.

A Note to My Readers

Dear Reader,

It is my hope that my story has touched and inspired you and given you a greater appreciation for life. My ordeal was difficult and challenging, but I believe that my trials and tribulations can have a positive impact on others

I would love to receive feedback from my readers and hear how my story has impacted their lives. I would also be happy to provide guidance and support through regular correspondence to anyone facing a similar situation.

Please contact me via email at
rivkahzucker@gmail.com

Thank you,
Rivkah Zucker

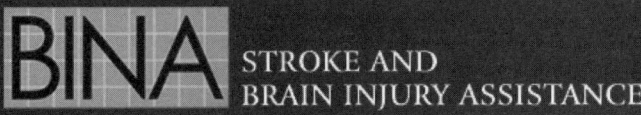
STROKE AND
BRAIN INJURY ASSISTANCE

About BINA

BINA Stroke and **B**rain **In**jury **A**ssistance is a nonprofit organization dedicated to the needs of individuals of all ages who have been affected by stroke and acquired brain injury, with a unique awareness of the needs of the Jewish population.

BINA guided me through the complex and overwhelming world of brain surgery rehabilitation and advised me of the latest and most effective therapies, which were instrumental in helping to accelerate my recovery. BINA's extensive research of rehabilitation options, wide array of support services and ongoing case management combine to provide crucial support for brain injury survivors to achieve all possible goals.

To contact BINA, call **718-645-6400**,
or visit their website at **www.BINAusa.org**.

Glossary

ad meah v'esrim shana	until one hundred and twenty years (of age)
ah freilichin Purim	Happy Purim
b'ahavah	with love
bar mitzvah	boy's thirteenth birthday
boruch Hashem	blessed is G-d
bayis ne'eman	trustworthy Jewish home
be'ezras Hashem	with G-d's help
becher	goblet
bedikas chametz	search for leaven (on the night preceding the eve of Pesach)
beis medrash	study hall
bentch licht	light Shabbos candles
bikur cholim	visiting the sick; also, an organization that assists the sick
birchos hashachar	blessings recited in the morning
bitachon	trust (in G-d)
brochah (-chos)	blessing(s)
bris	circumcision
challah (-llos)	traditional braided Shabbos bread(s)
chametz	leaven (not kosher for Pesach)
chas v'shalom	G-d forbid

chassan	groom
chasunah	wedding
chavrusah	study partner
chazak v'ematz	be strong and persevere
Chazal	our sages, of blessed memory
chessed	(acts of) kindness
chiyuv	obligation according to Jewish law
chizuk	strength, encouragement
chol hamoed	intermediate days of Sukkos and Pesach
cholent	traditional Shabbos stew
chuppah	marriage canopy
daven	pray
eiruv	an area, circumscribed by a symbolic line, within which carrying, forbidden on the Sabbath is permitted
eved	servant (of G-d)
erev	the day preceding a Shabbos or holiday
emunah	faith (in G-d)
fleishig	meat foods (Yiddish)
frum	religious, Torah observant (Yiddish)
g'zeirah	decree
gam zeh y'avar	this too shall pass
gadol	renowned rabbi

Glossary

geshikt(keit)	quick, efficient, domestically capable (Yiddish)
hachnassas orchim	hospitality
Haggadah	the story of the Exodus that is read during the Pesach *seder*
Hakadosh BoruchHu	the holy One, blessed is He (G-D)
hakaros hatov	appreciation, gratitude
hamotzie	blessing said on bread
halachah	Jewish law
hatzlachah	good luck, success
havdallah	ceremonial blessing said to mark the end of Shabbos
havtachah	promise
kallah	bride
kashrus	Jewish dietary laws
kiddush	blessing recited over wine before festive meals
kofer	heretic
kollel	learning program, usually for married men
kugel	Shabbos dish (Yiddish)
lein	read, especially from Jewish scripture (Yiddish)
mamash min haShamayim	truly heaven sent
matzah	unleavened bread
matzav	condition, circumstance
mechayil el chayil	from strength to strength

mechazeik	give other strength and encouragement
megillah	lit., scroll; often refers to the Scroll of Esther
middos	(good) character traits
milchig	dairy (Yiddish)
mishloach manos	gifts of food sent on Purim
Motzei Shabbos	Saturday night
nachas	pleasure or pride, usually from offspring
negel vasser	ritual washing of the hands upon awakening (Yiddish)
netilas yadayim	washing of the hands
nisayon	life test
pasuk, pesukim	verse(s)
peyos	side curls
Rebono shel olam	Master of the world (G-D)
refuah shleimah	complete recovery
siyata diShmaya	help from Heaven
seder (-darim)	festive Pesach meal that includes rituals and the reading of the Haggadah
seudah/seudos	festive meal(s)
shaitel	wig
shaliach (-luchim)	messenger(s)
shalosh seudos	third Shabbos meal
shema	primary prayer, also recited at bedtime

Glossary

shepping nachas	to garner pleasure or pride (Yiddish)
sheva berachos	festive meal during a couple's first week of marriage
shiur	Torah lecture
shmatas	rags (Yiddish)
shofar	ram's horn that is blown on Rosh Hashanah
shul	synagogue
shulchan aruch	festive meal during the Pesach *seder*
simchah (-chos)	joyous occasion(s)
talmid chacham	learned individual
tefillah	prayer
Tehillim	Psalms
Tatty	Father (Yiddish)
upsherin	boy's traditional first haircut at age three
vort	engagement party
Yaasher Koach	Thanks
Yiddishe	Jewish
Yiddishkeit	Judaism
yom(im) tov(im)	Jewish holiday(s)
zemiros	Shabbos songs
zocheh	worthy